Active Learning

THROUGH

Active Learning

THROUGH

Shirley Clarke

HODDER
EDUCATION
AN HACHETTE UK COMPANY

Also by Shirley Clarke:
Targeting Assessment in the Primary Classroom
Enriching Feedback in the Primary Classroom
Unlocking Formative Assessment
Formative Assessment in the Secondary Classroom
Formative Assessment in Action

Although every effort has been made to ensure that website addresses are correct at time of going to press, Hodder Education cannot be held responsible for the content of any website mentioned in this book. It is sometimes possible to find a relocated web page by typing in the address of the home page for a website in the URL window of your browser.

Hachette's policy is to use papers that are natural, renewable and recyclable products and made from wood grown in sustainable forests. The logging and manufacturing processes are expected to conform to the environmental regulations of the country of origin.

Orders: please contact Bookpoint Ltd, 130 Milton Park, Abingdon, Oxon OX14 4SB. Telephone: (44) 01235 827720. Fax: (44) 01235 400454. Lines are open 9.00–5.00, Monday to Saturday, with a 24-hour message answering service. Visit our website at www.hoddereducation.co.uk

Cover photos: Will & Deni McIntyre/Science Photo Library

Typeset in 11/13pt ITC Stone Informal by Servis Filmsetting Ltd, Stockport, Cheshire
Printed in Dubai

A catalogue record for this title is available from the British Library

ISBN 978 0 340 97445 2

Acknowledgements

I am indebted to the talented teachers who sent me examples of pupil work, pupil quotes and lesson descriptions for this book. I had far too many to include, but would like to express my appreciation. Your examples demonstrated the power of formative assessment. Thanks to the people whose work I was able to include:

Lynsey Atkins, St Martin's RC Primary School, East Lothian
Kathryn Atkinson, Collingwood Primary School, North Tyneside
Cath Ayles, Shinfield Junior School, Reading
Moira Bearwish, Damers First School, Dorset
Matthew Beresford, Stramongate Primary School, Cumbria
Emma Bradshaw, Earls Colne Primary School and Nursery, Essex
Glenys Bradshaw, Audley Junior School, Blackburn with Darwen
Nick Craven, Speyside High School, Moray
James Crump, Heron Way Primary School, Horsham, West Sussex
Gary Day-Lewis, Wentworth High School, Salford
Louise Edwards and Caroline Lane, Hallmoor School, Birmingham
Gillie van der Eyken, Southill Primary School, Dorset
Aurore Foti, George Stephenson High School, North Tyneside
Stella Gillett, Brecon High School, Powys
Sally Hunter, Wescott Infant School, Wokingham
Julie Jones, Mount Street Infant School, Powys
Lisa Naughton, Four Dwellings Primary School, Birmingham
Helen Rowley and Tracey Wheeler, Nunnery Wood Primary School, Birmingham
Charlotte Smith, North Hykeham Fosse Way Primary School, Lincoln
Bec Wakefield, Riverside Infant School, Essex
Melanie Watts, Brecon High School, Powys

My thanks go to Jenny Short, School Development Advisor for Bath and North East Somerset, together with Joy Mounter at Chew Stoke Primary School, and St Keyna Primary School, Keynsham, for their contributions to the key skills section in Chapter 6.

Thanks also to the fourteen learning teams from 2006 and 2007, whose findings are represented here. Your inspirational work will impact on many more pupils than in your own schools. Previous teams, Dorset and Gateshead, have also contributed to this book – thank you.

The 2006 teams:	The 2007 teams:
Blackburn with Darwen	Reading
East Lothian	Wokingham
Powys	North Tyneside
Gloucester	Glasgow
Essex	Birmingham
North Yorkshire	Moray
Salford	
Lincoln	

Special thanks to Emma Goff, Advanced Skills Teacher from Kent, Angi Gibson from New York Primary School in North Tyneside, Julie Oatridge from Hopeman Primary School in Moray, and Gerry Miller from the North Tyneside Education Action Zone for the excellent articles I persuaded them to write, and to Barry Silsby (School Improvement Partner, Croydon and East Sussex), Emma Goff and Tracy Goodway (Learning and Teaching Advisor, Essex) for comments on the manuscript.

Thank you, as always, to my editor Chas Knight for editing brilliance and for the colour!

Finally, my love and gratitude to:

My wonderful daughter Katy, for being so patient, brave and creative when Mummy was 'writing a book' and 'talking to the people'.

My equally wonderful but exhausted husband, John, for his loving support, for looking after Katy while I had my head down for weeks on end, for digitising all the realia for this book, and for creating 150 wonderful slides for my new presentations in a ridiculously short space of time.

Shirley Clarke

Website:
www.shirleyclarke-education.org – for information about various courses and for updates on Learning Team findings.

Contents

Introduction

I believe that my own journey in writing books about formative assessment in some way reflects the journey many teachers have taken over the last ten years. My first book, in 1998, focused on the very beginnings of formative assessment: getting away from continual summative assessment, sharing learning objectives, getting pupils to do some self-evaluation and improving teachers' marking. Over the last ten years, much of my focus has been on the detail of the essential techniques involved – how success criteria work for foundation subjects and how to get pupils to make their own improvements, and so on.

Today, although schools and teachers will always be at different stages of understanding and practice, things have evolved to a point where we can now perhaps fully integrate both principles and techniques. My last book, *Formative Assessment in Action: Weaving the elements together*, began the process of attempting to merge the thinking behind and the techniques involved in formative assessment *to create a coherent whole*. If the techniques are practised in isolation – as steps in a lesson, without an overriding rationale and mindset about the necessity of pupils being active participants in the learning process – then it just doesn't have the dramatic impact we know is possible. That book offered various whole lessons as examples of embedded formative assessment, with all its variations.

The aims for this book. . .

In compiling this book, I wanted to:

- make *active learning* the central focus;

- include the importance of a positive 'growth' mindset;

- include other good educational ideas and show how they link, to avoid the 'yet another thing to fit in' culture;

■ show how formative assessment fits the big picture of all assessment processes;

■ give as many examples of techniques in action as possible, across subjects and ages;

■ make the practical chapters work from both the teacher's and the pupil's points of view, aiming for a collaborative approach to learning;

■ enable schools and educational establishments to create their own learning teams, empowering them with the ability to independently and confidently develop formative assessment practice and thinking.

Why 'active learning'. . .?

This book takes the principle of *active learning as the heart of formative assessment* as the rationale for every chapter. Instead of formative assessment being 'done' to children, I am looking at teachers and pupils collaborating at all stages: in planning units of work, in deciding contexts for learning and success criteria, in analysing products for discussions about quality, in engaging in continual paired, or otherwise, classroom talk as a matter of course, in critically analysing learning as it is happening and engaging in a constant process of considered review of success and improvement. We want to 'make individuals active partners' in their learning (DfES, 2003, *Excellence and Enjoyment*): teachers and pupils as partners, and pupils as partners.

Pupil talk is the central feature of the classroom, the most significant element for pupils in enabling both an active learning environment, and the appropriate mindset to ensure that pupils see themselves as successful learners. Finally, the ability of teachers to shift the locus of control in the classroom from teacher to pupil – to 'let go' – is often the attitude change needed to make formative assessment successful and powerful.

As with anything of any worth in education, formative assessment has been argued over, misinterpreted and misused. One of the problems, I think, is that formative assessment needs to consist of some quite *specific techniques* while at the same time allowing for *experimentation and development*. A too-straitjacketed approach to techniques doesn't work because the underlying aims of active learning are not guiding the practice, requiring constant flexibility and re-evaluation of learning needs at the moment. A flexible, 'follow the principles and do your own thing' approach, however, leads to disillusionment when things don't work very well because the specifics of the techniques have not been studied. Both aspects make or break the success of formative assessment implementation. Thus, I have tried, in the following pages, to bring together what works in practice: specific techniques at their current cutting edge, with as many examples as I have room for, alongside continual references to the underlying thinking and aims of active learning.

Where the examples come from. . .

As always, I am indebted to the members of the action research learning teams I have worked closely with over the last two years, from whom I draw the wonderful examples of techniques in action throughout this book. There have been fourteen teams, each of thirty keen and talented teachers – 420 teachers in all – trialling and experimenting with initial starting points and their own ideas, and it is from them I have learnt the most about what is possible with formative assessment. The basic organisation of each team is as follows:

- Thirty keen and interested teachers, in pairs, from fifteen schools, make up the team.
- The team meets with me for three days, spread over a year.
- On Day 1, I present the teachers with current thinking, principles and current techniques, and they use these as starting points for their class-based action research.
- On Days 2 and 3, teachers feed back their findings, focusing on the impact on learning and evidence to back up their claims.
- Each teacher develops a special interest and 'showcases' that on the afternoon of Day 3.
- The feedback is written up and posted on my website, so that all learning teams – and anyone else – can access the details of their findings.

This book ends with a chapter on setting up a learning team in any educational setting, so the detail can be found there.

Sometimes the feedback from the teachers simply confirms what teachers in other teams have already found. . . sometimes the feedback takes the detail, and therefore understanding, of a particular technique or principle to a deeper level. . . and sometimes one teacher will have had a new, brilliant idea, which we all latch on to and teachers then trial before the next day. Sometimes one teacher's strategy for dealing with a problem will transform every teacher's practice. For example, in pairing talk partners, there were some teachers who did not know what to do with the extremely disruptive pupil who can't be paired with anyone. One teacher had found that if *she* became the child's partner, within three days the child was begging to be paired with a pupil, so powerful was the impact of exclusion from the peer group. The class discussions about ground rules and peer expectations and rights for talk partners resulted in a control of that pupil's behaviour which had not been seen before. I shared this finding with all the teams and it has become a universal technique for one aspect of the success of talk partners.

Also included. . .

I realise how easily teachers can fall into the trap of taking good things in education and following them slavishly so that other good things are then hard to integrate. I have tried to include references to ideas such as *thinking skills* and *building learning power* wherever appropriate, to help teachers see how inter-related these ideas are. In one lesson, or over time, all these can be happily integrated, because they are so compatible.

Finally, I have included information about summative assessment in one chapter, as a way of showing how formative assessment fits the big picture of all assessment.

Overview of the book

Chapter 1 revisits definitions, the history and purposes of formative assessment, with current thinking from recent research.

Chapter 2 places formative assessment in the context of *all* assessment.

Chapter 3 discusses the ideal learning culture and the role both teachers and pupils have in establishing it.

Chapter 4 focuses on pupil talk, the heart of formative assessment.

Chapter 5 explores what makes an effective and worthwhile question, and how we can get more out of questioning.

Chapter 6 deals with collaborative planning of units of work, including learning objectives and the contexts for the learning, as well as a key skills curriculum.

Chapter 7 looks at the importance of having 'pure' learning objectives.

Chapter 8 deals with the generation and use of success criteria.

Chapter 9 tackles the issue of quality and recognising excellence.

Chapter 10 discusses the ways in which self-, peer- and teacher evaluation and feedback can be embedded throughout lessons so that constant review and improvement become the norm.

Chapter 11 presents a model for setting up an action research learning team in any educational setting, with a contribution by an Advanced Skills Teacher giving her approach to helping teachers develop formative assessment.

Definitions, history and purposes of formative assessment

Why formative assessment?

Formative assessment is recognised as a significant strategy in raising pupil achievement – or indeed *any* learner's achievement. But *why* is raising achievement a continual quest for educators? Why are we never satisfied? The answer is that raising achievement is linked inextricably with individual quality of life and economic growth. Dylan Wiliam (2006) explains:

> ❝ It matters for individuals: there's no doubt that the higher the education level you have, the more you earn during your life, the longer you will live and the better your quality of life. For society, there are lower criminal justice costs; by increasing the level of education, you reduce the amount of money spent on incarcerating people. It reduces the cost of healthcare because people look after themselves better.

> '. . . if we could invest in education and raise student achievement by one standard deviation over 30 years, the extra growth in the economy, and the additional taxes paid by people just because they were so much richer, would mean that we wouldn't actually have to pay for education from reception up to age 18, because of all the extra money coming in. The developing countries and developed countries all realise this, so there are people on our tails and there is no alternative but to keep on raising levels of educational achievement. ❞

In order to be better learners, we know that pupils need to have higher-order thinking skills – skills which are transferable across different contexts within subjects and across different subjects. They also need generic, transferable *learning* skills. As Robert Fisher (1996a) says:

> ❝ Information is expanding at such a rate that individuals require transferable skills to enable them to address different problems in different contexts at different times throughout their lives. The

complexity of modern jobs requires people who can comprehend, judge and participate in generating new knowledge and processes. Modern democratic societies require its citizens to assimilate information from multiple sources, determine its truth and use it to make sound judgements. 〞

Black and Wiliam's 1998 review established that formative assessment leads to higher test results and therefore higher measurable pupil attainment – a key strategy for meeting economic need – but also helps pupils to become lifelong learners, with transferable skills: the educator's dream. From that moment, policy makers in England, and increasingly across the rest of the world, set the wheels in motion to make sure that formative assessment would gain as high a profile as possible – a move mostly welcomed by educators like myself, who were already spreading the word about the power of formative assessment.

What is the history of formative assessment?

In brief, the history of formative assessment is as follows (with thanks to Wiliam, 2006):

1967	Michael Scriven suggested the terms *formative* and *summative* to distinguish between different roles that evaluation might play. He said that formative evaluation *'might have a role in the on-going improvement of the curriculum'*.
1969	Benjamin Bloom applied the same terms and distinction to classroom tests. He said 'We see *much more effective use of formative evaluation if it is separated from the grading process and used primarily as an aid to teaching.'*
1987 and 1988	Natriello and Crooks published reviews of key studies involving formative assessment, providing clear evidence that classroom evaluation had substantial impact on students and their learning. Natriello (1987) identified the assessment cycle: purposes, setting of tasks, criteria and standards, evaluating performance and providing feedback. Crooks (1988) concluded that the summative function of assessment had been too dominant.
1998	Black and Wiliam were commissioned by the Assessment Reform Group (a group of academics) to review the literature about formative assessment between 1987 and 1997, in order to present their findings to policy makers in England. At that time, standard tests and other summative measures dominated. The review cited 250 studies and found that effective use of formative assessment yielded improvements in student achievement between 0.4 and 0.7 standard deviations and was likely to lead to lifelong learning.

What do all the different terms used today mean?

Formative assessment is generally known in England as *Assessment for Learning*. In Scotland there is *Assessment **of** Learning*, *Assessment **for** Learning* and *Assessment **as** Learning*, all tied together as *Assessment is for learning*. These three form perhaps the most accurate way of distinguishing between different types of assessment. That is:

- **Assessment OF learning** is any summative test or assessment, whether class-based, school-based or national (e.g. a national test, a GCSE or a recall question such as *'How many wives did Henry VIII have?'* or *'Which are the odd numbers between 2 and 10?'*).

- **Assessment FOR learning** is any practice which provides information to pupils about what to do to improve (e.g. *'This adjective could be better'*).

- **Assessment AS learning** is any practice which takes the 'what to improve' into 'how to improve' (e.g. *'Think about your senses'*, *'Use our adjective bank'*, *'Look at this paragraph using effective adjectives from a child last year'*).

My work focuses on *assessment for* and *as learning*, and as the primary goal of *assessment for learning* is that *assessment as learning* should result, I prefer to keep things simple by sticking to the term *formative assessment* to describe both elements!

What are the key messages related to formative assessment?

In 2002, the Assessment Reform Group published the following ten principles:

❝ *Formative assessment:*

- *is part of effective planning;*
- *focuses on how pupils learn;*
- *is central to classroom practice;*
- *is a key professional skill;*
- *is sensitive and constructive;*
- *fosters motivation;*

*   *promotes understanding of goals and criteria;*
*   *helps learners know how to improve;*
*   *develops the capacity for self- and peer-assessment;*
*   *recognises all educational achievement.* '

They listed the seven 'key characteristics' of formative assessment as follows:

' *Formative assessment:*

*   *is embedded in a view of teaching and learning of which it is an essential part;*
*   *involves sharing learning goals with pupils;*
*   *aims to help pupils to know and to recognise the standards they are aiming for;*
*   *involves pupils in self- and peer-assessment;*
*   *provides feedback which leads to pupils recognising their next steps and how to take them;*
*   *promotes confidence that every pupil can improve;*
*   *involves both teacher and pupils reviewing and reflecting on assessment data (and information).* '

In the spirit of inevitable development of our understanding, Dylan Wiliam (2006) argues that there are now five key strategies involved in formative assessment:

' *   *clarifying and understanding learning intentions and criteria for success;*
*   *engineering effective classroom discussions, questions and tasks that elicit evidence of learning;*
*   *providing feedback that moves learners forward;*
*   *activating students as teaching and learning resources for each other;*
*   *activating students as owners of their own learning.* '

My own current thinking is that there are seven strategies involved in formative assessment – of course overlapping Wiliam's five – and each strategy is carried out through a number of techniques. The strategies hardly change over time, whereas the techniques are developing continually.

Key strategies involved in formative assessment

■ Creating a classroom culture in which all involved see ability as incremental rather than fixed.

■ Involving pupils in planning both appropriately pitched content and meaningful contexts.

■ Clarifying learning objectives and establishing pupil-generated and therefore pupil-owned success criteria.

■ Enabling and planning effective classroom dialogic talk and worthwhile questioning.

■ Involving pupils in analysis and discussion about what excellence consists of – not just the meeting of success criteria, but *how* to best meet them.

■ Enabling pupils to be effective self- and peer-evaluators.

■ Establishing continual opportunities for timely review and feedback from teachers and pupils, focusing on recognition of success and improvement needs, and provision of time to act on that feedback.

These strategies for formative assessment provide both teachers and learners with the framework with which to steer the decisions made about tasks and techniques. The techniques change and there are often many ways to fulfil a strategy, but the principles need to be constant and the basis of school consistency. Techniques will often be different from teacher to teacher, and necessarily so for different age groups, but it is the strategies and principles which create our ultimate frame of reference for effective practice.

The acid test of effective formative assessment, however, is not how well written the strategies are, or how many good techniques are in use, but the extent to which pupils are, as a result of our work, actively engaged in thinking, learning and assessing that learning.

2 The link with summative assessment: long-, medium- and short-term assessment

> Summative assessment must be in harmony with the procedures of formative assessment and should be designed to minimise the burden on teachers and pupils.

This was the welcome key message to teachers from the Assessment Reform Group in 2006. They then listed the following **implications for school management**:

> - Establish a school policy for assessment that supports assessment for learning at all times and requires summative assessment only when necessary for checking and reporting progress.
>
> - Arrange quality assurance of all summative assessment, including any tests given by teachers, so that decisions made within a school about the progress of pupils are based on dependable information.
>
> - Ensure that parents understand how assessment is helping learning and how criteria are used in reporting progress at given times during the year.
>
> - Resist pressure for "hard" data from tests and encourage use of a range of types of evidence of pupil's learning.
>
> - Provide protected time for quality assurance of teachers' assessment through moderation.

Implications for teachers were as follows:

> - Ensure that assessment is always used to help learning and that, when a summative assessment report is needed, the best evidence is reliably judged against relevant criteria.

- *Involve pupils in self-assessment of ongoing work and help them to understand the criteria used in assessing their work for reporting purposes and how summative judgements are made.*

- *Take part in moderation of summative judgements and other quality assurance procedures.*

- *Use tests only when most appropriate, not as routine.* **9**

(Assessment Reform Group, 2006)

The biggest problem today about summative tracking for schools in England, and maybe elsewhere, appears to be that many inspectors want electronic data which they can use to make judgements about the effectiveness of a school. Since the advent of quick inspections, they often do not have time to delve into the source of the judgements, or to see what is happening to meet the needs of pupils not 'on track'. This has led many schools to create electronic data for mainly accountability reasons. As with feedback information, it is only worthwhile if it is acted upon, so there is nothing wrong with electronic data, or any other kind, *if it used to further pupil learning.* Yet time is often being spent creating sheets of numbers and statistics rather than *using* gathered information to make a difference to individual pupils' learning.

In order to look at some solutions and to place formative assessment appropriately, it is useful to trace assessment practice from the long term to the short term. Typical effective processes in place at each stage are outlined.

Long-term assessment

Most *summative* assessment focuses on the longer term. Pupil progress is summarised to meet a variety of purposes: reporting to parents, supporting transition to next teacher or school, and certification of learning through exams.

Schools typically use whole-school performance data, from in school or out, to evaluate how well the school is doing, especially regarding curriculum, learning and teaching issues pinpointed by the data. Decisions made about the needs arising are fed back into medium- and short-term planning. Numerical data is only one part of the evidence used for analysis. It would be important, for instance, to regularly collect work samples for whole-school analysis, to make sure teachers' judgements are dependable and to see the patterns of attainment and progress.

Medium-term assessment

Pupil progress is reviewed at intervals, perhaps termly, so that teachers can decide, for each pupil, whether they are 'on track' and make sure something is done about those who are not. 'On track' seems to make sense, for a class, if linked to level expectations. If pupils are achieving the objectives from the current year as they encounter/experience them through the taught curriculum, then they are on track for national expectations. If they are working very confidently on the current ones, and in addition are working on some from the next year, they are beyond expectations for the year group in those areas. Similarly, if they are working on objectives from earlier years, they are working below expectations for the year group. Where pupils are working below expectations, a teacher would need to provide sound evidence of previous attainment in order to indicate that progress had been made. For individuals, 'on track' is increasingly focused on whether progress has been made, rather than simply meeting age-related expectations.

What matters is that individual children need to be doing as well as they can be doing, and those who are standing still – especially in the key areas of literacy and numeracy – need to be identified and discussed. All this sounds daunting, but we need to make sure that *every* pupil has the right to progress, without giving ourselves the burden of accountability exercises which have no impact on individual children's progress.

Targets are often set as part of performance management: teachers are rewarded for how well their pupils do. It seems most appropriate to start from each individual pupil's current level and determine what would be a positive target for that pupil in terms of the progress he/she might make. Many targets will not be reached, but setting a target which is optimistic usually leads to teachers having higher expectations, and to pupils doing better than they would have with a 'safe' target. Problems occur, of course, when targets which are too ambitious lead teachers to teach to the test.

It is expected that teachers monitor progress regularly enough to be able to see how far the class as a whole is 'on track' and where individual pupils are not. The most obvious method of determining current attainment would be to take a sample of unaided writing, to hear the child read and so on, and determine a level for that child's performance. This should confirm what the teacher already knows from ongoing classroom work, but ensures that individual children's progress is monitored and that something is actually *done* if children – whether high or low achievers – are not making appropriate progress.

Keeping some kind of school-wide or school-generated table which plots levels, or sub-levels, for children over time means a pupil who is not making progress will be obvious. Alternatively, if levels are recorded on an annual basis, teachers and school leaders would need to find some other way of making sure pupils do not have to wait till the end of the year for appropriate teaching intervention.

In order for teachers to make reliable judgements about ongoing progress, regular moderation meetings are necessary, where all staff analyse collections of work against level descriptions and decide on a common interpretation of 'best fit'. Additionally, effective heads, or other senior managers, have regular meetings with teachers, often once a term, in which every pupil is discussed individually. It is only through this face-to-face contextualised discussion that every pupil can be guaranteed a time when their needs will be considered.

There will always be some pupils who are lower achievers and some who are higher, but the point of all this is to monitor progress for *all* pupils and to *do* something about individual pupils if they are not making enough progress.

So what can be done when a pupil is not making enough progress? First off all, possible reasons for the lack of progress need to be discussed, such as whether any external factors are affecting progress. In most cases, underachievement at any level is because of ineffective teaching for those pupils. This does not mean that the teaching is ineffective for all learners, but that issues such as how to give all pupils access to classroom tasks, or how to make tasks sufficiently challenging for higher achievers who are not making progress, need to be considered. A teacher who has embedded formative assessment – with pupils owning and monitoring their own work and progress against success criteria, discussing their learning with their peers and understanding what excellence looks like – is likely to be meeting the needs of every individual pupil.

We can now look at the short-term stage, where formative assessment comes into play. Formative assessment is the means for providing the best learning environment possible for all pupils.

Short-term assessment

Assessment becomes formative when it gives practical and explicit advice which will help learners know how to improve – deepening and furthering their understanding, thinking and learning.

Formative assessment takes place, therefore, at the short term: embedded in day-to-day lessons, often described as the learning itself. It consists of the following strategies, already stated on page 10, but useful to revisit here, alongside long- and short-term assessment.

Key strategies involved in formative assessment

- Creating a classroom culture in which all involved see ability as incremental rather than fixed.

- Involving pupils in planning both appropriately pitched content and meaningful contexts.

- Clarifying learning objectives and establishing pupil-generated (and therefore pupil-owned) success criteria.

- Enabling and planning effective classroom dialogic talk and worthwhile questioning.

- Involving pupils in analysis and discussion about what excellence consists of – not just the meeting of success criteria, but *how* best to meet them.

- Enabling pupils to be effective self- and peer-evaluators.

- Establishing continual opportunities for timely feedback from teachers and pupils, focusing on recognition of success and improvement needs, and provision of time to act on that feedback.

For further excellent advice and some useful questions for teachers, assessment leaders, curriculum leaders/heads of departments and senior managers about summarising, recording and tracking progress, I recommend the Birmingham Advisory and Support Service (BASS) Assessment Unit publication *Effective Assessment: summarising, recording and tracking progress* (Birmingham City Council, 2007). It is a large, fold-out card, accessible, clear and entirely focused on the aims of the Assessment Reform Group's key messages stated at the beginning of this chapter.

Reflection

- How much time is spent levelling pupil attainment?
- What do you use as periodic snapshot evidence?
- Are the levels/sub-levels interpreted consistently across all teachers?
- Are there regular moderation meetings to ensure consistency?
- Is the summative tracking worthwhile? Does it enable pupils who are standing still or slow-moving to be checked and discussed, or is it done to give data to inspectors?
- Are there regular meetings with each teacher to discuss all pupils' progress?
- Are the intervention strategies for getting pupils back 'on track' evaluated regularly and revisited if proving unsuccessful?
- Is there a distinction made between 'on track' for a class or cohort and 'on track' for each individual pupil?

3 The ideal learning culture

6 *Motivation is the most important factor in determining whether you succeed in the long run. What I mean by motivation is not only the desire to achieve, but also the love of learning, the love of challenge and the ability to thrive on obstacles. These are the greatest gifts we can give our students.* 9

(Dweck, 2006)

Over the years during which our understanding and practice of formative assessment have so far evolved, it has been clear that strategies and techniques have very little impact if the *culture of the classroom* does not support the philosophy or ethos of the key principles. We can list the component parts or key messages of formative assessment, but the appropriate learning culture consists of less tangible elements. The elements which most often arise in discussion in my learning teams and in other continuing research are dealt with in this chapter. What seems to matter the most are:

■ How teachers and pupils view ability and consequently their learning potential;

■ What teachers and pupils think the ideal learning environment should consist of, and effective strategies to create and sustain that learning culture.

How teachers and pupils view ability and their learning potential

Much research carried out by Carol Dweck and others (e.g. Dweck, 1975, Weiner, 1984; Weiner, Heckhausen and Meyer, 1972) shows that pupils differ in whether they regard their successes and failures as the result of certain factors. Boys are more likely to attribute their successes to ability and their failures to lack of effort and bad luck. Girls, on the other hand, are more likely to attribute their successes to effort and their failures to lack of ability. Girls, especially, if they feel unsuccessful, are liable to suffer from low confidence which, if it continues, results in what Dweck (1975) calls 'learned helplessness'.

Dweck built on this work and has now established – through thirty years of studies involving thousands of children and adults from all walks of life – that what matters the most, in terms of motivation, is whether we see ability as *fixed* (an entity learner) or *growth* (an incremental learner). In short, people with a 'fixed' mindset will only tackle tasks which they know, in advance, they will succeed at. People with a 'growth' mindset not only willingly tackle difficult tasks, but thrive on them. Examples of both mindsets, in terms of their characteristics and the repercussions, are given below. Our aim, of course, must be to develop a *growth* mindset – for ourselves, for all adults involved in working with children, for parents and all our pupils.

The 'fixed' mindset

Characteristics of a 'fixed' mindset	Repercussions
My intelligence is a fixed trait – I have a certain amount of it and that's that.	I worry about how much intelligence I have and it makes me interested in looking and feeling as if I have enough. I must look clever and, at all costs, not look stupid.
I feel clever when things are easy, where I put in little effort and I outperform my peers.	Effort, difficulty, setbacks or higher performing peers call my intelligence into question, even if I have high confidence in my intelligence, so I feel stupid.
I need easy successes to feel clever.	Challenges are a threat to my self-esteem, so I won't engage with them.
I don't want to have my inadequacies and errors revealed.	I will withdraw from valuable learning opportunities if I think this might happen.
Even if I'm doing well initially, I won't be able to cope with a problem or obstacle.	I readily disengage from tasks when obstacles occur.

The 'growth' mindset

Characteristics of a 'growth' mindset	Repercussions
Intelligence is something I can increase through my own efforts.	I am keen to work hard and learn as much as I can.
I acknowledge that there are differences between people in how much they know and how quickly they master things.	I believe that everyone, with effort and guidance, can increase their intellectual abilities.
I love to learn something new.	I will readily sacrifice opportunities to look clever in favour of opportunities to learn something new.
I am excited by challenge.	Even if I have low confidence in my intelligence, I throw myself into difficult tasks – and stick with them. I set myself goals and make sure I have strategies to reach them.
I feel clever when . . .	I am fully engaged with a new task, exerting effort to master something, stretching my skills and putting my knowledge to good use (e.g. helping other pupils learn).

People with a fixed mindset need to constantly prove their ability, proving that they are special or even superior, whereas people with a growth mindset believe that intelligence can be developed through learning – something which brain research has proved to be true. In one study (Dweck, 2006), people were asked hard questions and given feedback about their answers. Their brain waves were monitored to see where they were interested and attentive. People with a fixed mindset were only interested when the feedback reflected their ability, when they were told whether they were right or wrong. When they were presented with information which could help them learn, they showed no sign of interest, even when given the right answer for something they had got wrong. Only people with a growth mindset paid close attention to information that could stretch their knowledge. For them, learning was a priority. Even for people with a growth mindset, failure can still be painful, but the big difference between them and people with a fixed mindset is that they don't believe that failure *defines* you. It is rather a problem to be faced, dealt with and learnt from.

Self-esteem

Before I outline strategies for encouraging a growth mindset in ourselves and our pupils, we need to be clear about our understanding of self-esteem. All parents, hopefully, want their children to have a basic sense of self-worth – to know that they have our respect and love, but after that self-esteem is something *they* are in charge of and we can only facilitate. High self-esteem happens for those with a growth mindset when they are using their abilities to the fullest in something they value, rather than showing that they are better than someone else.

Strategies for developing a growth mindset – for teachers, parents and all involved in education

Modelling a growth mindset

We need to model our own growth mindset and love of learning by emphasising processes of learning, the importance and excitement of meeting challenges, putting in effort and using strategies which help us learn. We need to teach children that intelligence can be developed. We need to transform 'difficulty' into 'new or deeper learning' and avoid expressing sympathy when children encounter failure or difficulty. We need to show enthusiasm about challenging tasks and ensure that failure is followed up by celebration of what has been learnt by the experience, in terms of new strategies needed. By doing this, we help ensure that challenge and effort are things that *enhance* self-esteem rather than threaten it.

Teachers with a fixed mindset often give lower achievers less demanding work in order to preserve their self-esteem – making sure they succeed, telling them how clever they are . . . and dooming them to fall further behind. This approach also ensures that these pupils will only feel successful when they can do things easily.

With a growth mindset, you tell pupils the truth. If they don't have skills or knowledge, or if they are underachieving, this is not a sign of something shameful, but a sign that they need to work harder or be helped to find new strategies. By giving pupils greater access to tasks (i.e. increasing the level of support within the task itself), for instance, they instantly have greater access to the success criteria used in formative assessment.

Praising effort and achievement rather than ability or personal attributes

Praising pupils' intelligence harms their motivation and their performance. Children love to be praised for their intelligence and talent, but if this is the norm, the minute they encounter an obstacle their confidence drops. If success means they are clever, then failure can only mean they are not! This hooks them neatly into a fixed mindset. Dweck (2006) gives some examples of well-meaning comments and what pupils actually hear:

'You learned that so quickly! You're so clever!
If I don't learn something quickly I'm not clever.

'Look at that drawing! Is he the next Picasso or what?'
I shouldn't try drawing anything hard or they'll see I'm not.

'You're so brilliant! You got an A without even studying!'
I'd better stop studying or they won't think I'm brilliant.'

Any feedback we give pupils clearly needs to support a view of ability as incremental rather than fixed. We need to praise pupils for **what they have accomplished** and **the strategies used**, such as practice, research, persistence, evaluating and making improvements: *'Well done, that is a beautiful rainbow, especially the way you've worked so carefully at blending the colours', 'Fantastic. You worked so hard at that problem.'*

With my own three-year-old daughter, I have been able to see at first hand the impact of the language used to encourage and praise. Before I read *Mindset*, by Dweck, I was more likely to absent-mindedly tell her how clever she was at all her infant achievements, like crawling and walking. Luckily, those things are now mastered and are no longer part of a learning journey. When she first completed an easy jigsaw, however, I again told her how clever she was – and saw the exact repercussions described by Dweck. The moment she now encounters any form of difficulty with a jigsaw, she expresses displeasure and says *'You do it!'* She refuses to have a go if I tell her to try again. We now only use the word *clever* to describe something inanimate, rather then to describe her ability (*'The way that hot air balloon works is so clever'*) and again, she copies our use of the word (*'That's clever! The cooker rings a bell!'*). I have found it particularly effective to focus my praise on learning, telling her how good it is that she is *learning to* . . . write, read, use paints, cut out, use a potty, etc. She copies this language about things she still has to work at, with pride and enthusiasm (*'Look Daddy! I am learning to wind the tape measure'*). The words we use clearly form attitudes and beliefs.

So what *do* you say when someone completes something quickly and perfectly? At home, you would just acknowledge that it had been achieved, with no mention of any related intelligence. Dweck states that speed and perfection are the enemy of difficult learning, so, in the classroom, we would respond by apologising for wasting their time in giving them something which was not challenging enough. Children need further learning experiences, rather than to do things they find easy.

A set of commonly devised strategies for dealing with challenge can be a useful visual prompt for enabling pupils to be self-sufficient, such as:

When something really makes you think . . .

1. Don't worry or panic.
2. Remind yourself that, if it makes you think, you are learning.
3. Read the success criteria again and check exactly where you are having difficulties.
4. Look at any finished examples to see what other pupils have done.
5. Ask your talk partner for advice.
6. Use class resources to help solve the problem, such as a thesaurus or number line.

Avoiding external rewards

The fixed mindset is perpetuated by the use of external rewards, mistakenly given to pupils to boost their self-esteem, when the opposite actually results. A considerable number of studies (e.g. Dweck, 1989; Elliot and Dweck, 1988) show that *performance goals* – such as house points, gold stars, class ranking or comparison with others, smiley faces, wanting to win positive judgements about your performance, and so on – lead to pupils who:

■ avoid challenge when they have doubts about their ability compared with others;

■ tend to create an excuse for failure;

■ tend to see ability as fixed;

■ concentrate much of their task analysis on gauging the difficulty of the task and calculating their chances of gaining favourable ability judgements;

■ attribute difficulty to low ability;

■ give up in the face of difficulty;

■ become upset when faced with difficulty or failure.

Lepper and Hodell (1989) found that external rewards have a detrimental effect on intrinsic motivation. Extrinsic rewards can be seen as a 'bribe' which skew motivation. They adversely affect performance, encouraging pupils to complete tasks as quickly as possible, and include only those features which are needed in order to gain the reward. Children who are used to rewards tend in future not to choose activities where there are no rewards to be had, and also prefer less demanding tasks. Intrinsic motivation, or a growth mindset, promotes more effective, deeper and longer-lasting learning.

Gerry Miller, the coordinator of the North Tyneside Learning Team for 2007, was particularly interested in the implications of fixed and growth mindsets and had introduced teachers to Carol Dweck's work before the team first met. As a result of the extra experimentation in schools which stemmed from this focus, I asked both Gerry and one of the teachers involved in working with her class on developing a growth mindset to write about their findings for this book. Gerry Miller's interesting account is given first, followed by Angi Gibson's, a Deputy Head and Year 6 teacher (11 year olds).

The importance of a growth mindset in raising achievement and aspirations

Gerry Miller, North Tyneside EAZ director

When I came across Carol Dweck's research in her book *Self-Theories: Their Role in Motivation, Personality & Development* (2000), I realised that we need to overtly promote the growth mindset if we are to develop truly resilient, self-sufficient learners.

If I had known of Carol Dweck's work when I was teaching in secondary schools, I would have said to the bottom set I used to teach something like this:

'This is set 3 out of three. You are in this group mainly because of some poor literacy skills. We are going to work extra hard to improve your literacy skills at the same time as we learn about history, and have some fun along the way. We are going to do the same work as the higher sets, and our aim is to do better than many of those in set 2. If you achieve that, you will have the chance to move up. The best way for us to be successful is to work together and support each other so that everyone will be successful.'

It was interesting to note that, when asked what these students found useful in lessons, they often said things like: *'Learning how to spell key words as I'm not a good speller'* or *'Learning where to put the apostrophe'*. This was useful feedback to me, as it told me that they valued help with literacy skills and recognised this was where they needed to improve the most.

In my dealings with pupils now, mainly Year 5 and 6 (10 and 11 year olds), I use the following strategies to encourage 'fixed mindset' learners to become 'growth mindset' learners:

1. Ask children to discuss with talk partners **what we mean by intelligence**.

   Some will come up with **fixed mindset ideas**, such as:
   * *How smart you are.*
   * *Inborn ability to learn complex ideas.*
   * *The ability to survive with the least effort while still doing really well.*

   Others will come up with **growth mindset ideas**, such as:
   * *Studying hard.*
   * *The amount of knowledge you possess and how you use it.*
   * *How much effort you put into something.*

2. Ask them when they **feel smart**:

   Fixed mindset ideas:
   * *When I don't make mistakes.*
   * *When I finish my work first.*
   * *When I get easy work.*

   Growth mindset ideas:
   * *When I don't know how to do it and it's pretty hard and I figure it out without anyone telling me.*
   * *When I'm doing school work because I want to learn to get smart.*
   * *When I'm reading a hard book.*

3. Use Dweck's list of **characteristics of the different mindsets** to stimulate discussion with children on what it means to be an Entity Learner or an Incremental Learner.

4. Explain how the view on **intelligence** has changed over the last ten years – many people used to think it was fixed, but most educationists now see it as something that can be changed through learning.

5. Discuss the **importance of challenge** and having a go at difficult tasks – we shouldn't be afraid to get things wrong, because that's how we learn. If work is easy, it means we are not learning – if it's hard, we need to keep trying, as that is how we learn.

6. Discuss **role models** with children of people who have achieved success through hard work. Children often equate success with innate ability rather than hard work and imagine that clever or skilful people can be successful without working hard. An example is English footballer Alan Shearer – not considered one of the most skilful players when he was in junior teams, but very hard-working, determined and focused: he believed he would succeed and was prepared to put the effort in to get there.

7. Discuss possible **pressures on us not to work hard**. Some people think it is 'cool' not to work hard. These people are unlikely to achieve much. 'Swot' is a four-letter word!

8. Discuss the **importance of resilience**. Many children want to give up when the work gets hard, or want the teacher or Teaching Assistant to come and help them as soon as they get stuck. The more they can learn to use a variety of strategies to overcome difficulties without help from an adult, the more they are likely to succeed in more difficult tasks as they get older. We should celebrate mistakes and praise those who stick at a task and don't give up.

9. **Compare our brain with our muscles** – the more we use it, the stronger it gets.

10. **When we move up to High School** it will help if we are incremental learners because:

   - *We will probably find some subjects harder than others. It is important that we don't give up when we find it hard.*
   - *We will be out of the 'comfort zone' of our primary classroom – this is when those with a fixed mindset sometimes struggle.*
   - *We will have lots of different teachers – we want to show them that we are willing to have a go, and that we don't need an adult to help us whenever the work gets difficult.*

Becoming Incremental Learners

Angi Gibson – Deputy Head at New York Primary School, North Tyneside

New York Primary is recognised as being within a super output area of deprivation, with the highest percentage of NEETs (16–18 year olds Not in Education, Employment or Training) recorded. Once pupils enter education they soon assume an attitude that they are as they are, and what we see is as good as it gets. These low aspirations are confirmed within the family, often supported by anecdotes that mother, father, brother and sister were also 'no good' at school – and so the myth perpetuates. This mindset must be challenged, as the school faces a raising standards agenda.

With my Year 6 class, it became clear that until some of my pupils' self-worth and personal capacity issues were tackled, success and achievement would remain out of their reach.

I first asked my pupils to complete the *Implicit Theories of Intelligence Scale for Children – Self-Form* questionnaire, included by Carol Dweck in her book *Self-theories* (2000). The results, as of September 2006, were as we feared: **only 18% of the class had a growth mindset, 11% were borderline and 71% had a fixed mindset**. These results were proof of the need to change!

I began my journey by realising very quickly that there was **NO** one-step method to success! I found that the best way to promote the growth mindset with my children was through an amalgamation of various strategies.

The techniques that I used to implement change were first and foremost:

1. **Building self-esteem and belief in self-ability**

2. Reinforcing and encouraging steps of learning

3. Celebrating an awareness of self-recognition

These three strategies were promoted and adopted through using the following teaching techniques:

- Target setting (SMART)
- Peer teaching (buddies)
- Assessment for learning
- Meaningful praise – recognising how their learning was moving on
- Recognising wrong answers as being a positive thing, something to learn from
- The 5 R's for learning: Resilience, Responsibility, Resourcefulness, Reasoning and Reflectivity-Reflexivity (Smith and Call, 1999)
- Less teacher talk – more pupil talk
- Positive self-narrative and visualisation
- Increasing roles of responsibility within and around school through increasing the pupils' sense of belonging, self-worth and importance
- Managing the moment of impulse – good questioning techniques, etc
- Problem-solving, mind-mapping/templates, hierarchy of questions
- Collecting facts before making judgements
- Regular review, post-analysis of work and emphasis on perfect practice.

I began to record our incremental learning journey into a checklist:

- Goal-setting through visualisation
- Using all data to target-set for incremental improvement
- Share and negotiate the curriculum with the pupils
- Give parents knowledge of the curriculum (in parent speak)
- Share national curriculum targets with pupils and parents
- Use posters and visual resources as aids for incremental learning
- Check regularly how familiar pupils are with content of posters
- Realistic tests practice throughout the year
- Teach skills of how to mark and assess own work (learning/success criteria)
- Talk about emotions during learning and tests
- Teach relaxation and have a range of movements and/or techniques (brain gym/take 10/activate body and mind)
- Use music for mood and atmosphere
- Morale-boosting self-talk before tests
- Celebrate all successes.

Through training, the majority of my pupils were noted to be incremental learners when re-tested in January 2007. The results were as follows:

- 85% growth mindset
- 4% borderline
- 11% fixed mindset

The effect of this on their learning was phenomenal! The majority of my pupils were now totally tuned into learning – hungry for it, even. They were no longer just content with finishing a piece of work: it had to challenge them. Their newly-found learning goals and standards enabled them to think like an incremental learner. Their mindset is now:

- I thrive on challenge
- I throw myself into difficult tasks
- I am self-confident
- I have learning goals
- I like feedback on my performance so that I can improve
- I react to failure by trying harder
- I engage in self-monitoring
- I can ignore the low aspirations of my peers
- I believe that intelligence is not fixed
- My intelligence can be improved through learning.

What was truly amazing was the fact that I, the teacher, was seen as the last resort (instead of the first) that the pupils would approach for help. The first was now their buddy, then their table buddies, and finally the teaching and non-teaching staff. It freed us up tremendously! It gave us the time that we once never had, yet should have had, to guide and keep the pupils on track.

Due to the changes implemented, the pupils absolutely thrived upon the programme: their confidence and self-belief was overwhelming, they were not scared of challenges any more – they were welcoming them! They were learners with a growth mindset!

What the ideal learning environment should consist of, and effective strategies to create and sustain it

Wiliam (2006) states that the key features of an effective learning environment are that it creates **pupil engagement** and it is **well-regulated**. In the context of learning, *well-regulated* refers to **guiding learning to the appropriate goal**. We can also add to this the importance of **dialogue and active reflection**.

Active pupil engagement is an indicator of real learning taking place. Pupils learn best when they have a slightly difficult task which they have to work at (Vygotsky's *'zone of proximal development'*, 1978), which leads them into a state of 'flow'. Knowing they can cope with difficulties makes pupils seek challenges and overcome further problems. *'Flow'* is an interesting term which usefully describes how engaged a person is in an activity, the level of absorption, how rapt or engaged they are in their learning (Claxton, 2002).

Establishing the requirements for learning

In order to ensure effective engagement, reflection, dialogue and appropriate guidance, we need to create, with pupils, the best environment for those elements and therefore for effective learning to take place. As with all formative assessment, pupils need to be actively involved in deciding, with teachers, what they need.

The best place to start exploring the ideal learning environment is by talking to pupils about their lives and their learning. This is Diana Pardoe's (2005) advice in her publication *Towards Successful Learning*, which I recommend as an excellent resource for this purpose. Her work involves a model of successful learning, synthesising formative assessment and the Critical Skills Programme as well as her own substantial work with teachers and pupils. Following her aim of *'teachers and learners engage together in high-quality learning conversations'*, she suggests the following questions are asked of pupils to begin the process of establishing a positive climate for learning:

1. *What do you want your teacher to be like?*
2. *What do you want the classroom to be like?*
3. *So what are you going to do (in order to enable your teacher and classroom to be as you wish)?*

Pupils could decide the answers to these questions alone, through jottings, through talk partners – and then, critically, the answers must be *shared* so that everyone can see them and a class list of answers established.

The next step is for pupils to work in small groups to identify what *helps* them to learn (movers) and what *stops* them from learning (blockers).

What helps you learn? (Three minutes to brainstorm ideas and a further three minutes to discuss and then prioritise the top three ideas from the group.)

What stops you from learning? (Again, three minutes to brainstorm ideas and a further three minutes to discuss and then prioritise the top three ideas from the group.)
 It is very important that those engaged in this activity respond to the questions from their own perspective as learners. For example, when teachers are working together, they need to consider how they feel as adult learners, not how they think the children in their classes feel about learning. From the lists created, group members then explore together what successful learners do (see Fig. 3.1).
 It is important that the question is phrased *'What does a successful learner do?'* so that the responses given include a verb, such as *listens, thinks, tries hard, asks questions* or *reads*. This emphasises that specific actions are required to become successful in learning. From the verbs used, specific observable behaviours can then be identified that illustrate the action. For example:

You have said that a successful learner listens.
What does that look like/sound like in our classroom/staffroom/school?

You have said that a successful learner takes care of things.
What does that look like/sound like in our classroom setting?

You have said that a successful learner makes sure he/she understands what to do.
What does that look like/sound like in our classroom/school?

(reproduced from Pardoe, 2005, by kind permission of Continuum)

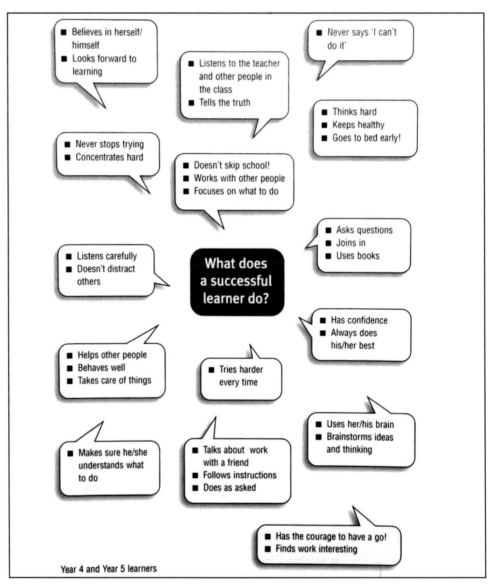

Fig. 3.1 Children's responses (from Pardoe, 2005)

Taking it further: learning how to learn

Pupils

Much research has been done in the last decade about the importance of pupils learning about learning, or *meta-cognition*. **Pupils need not only the ideal learning environment, but also the skills to be able to control their own learning**.

David Hargreaves (2004) outlined three significant gateways to 'personalised learning': student voice, assessment for learning and learning to learn. He defines 'student voice' as: *'How students come to play a more active role in their education and schooling as a result of teachers becoming more attentive, in sustained or routine ways, to what students say about their experience of learning and of school life.'*

In Chapter 4 there are a number of quotes from pupils about their experiences and opinions of having talk partners. They are excellent examples of pupils actively exercising 'student voice'.

Guy Claxton's (2002) book *Building Learning Power* is well known amongst teachers for his four learning-power dispositions:

> **Resilience**: absorption, managing distractions, noticing and perseverance
> **Resourcefulness**: questioning, making links, imagining, reasoning and capitalising
> **Reflectiveness**: planning, revising, distilling and meta-learning
> **Reciprocity**: interdependence, collaboration, empathy and listening, imitation

In order to become higher-order thinkers in a modern world, Claxton believes children need to be helped to develop the power of learning in these four areas. In analysing the four areas, I was able to link them all with different aspects of formative assessment:

- **Resilience**: the ethos of an incremental mindset and engagement as active learners.

- **Resourcefulness**: talk partners, effective formative questions to pupils which result in high-quality thinking and discussion; pupils engaged in peer- and self-evaluation and class analysis of what constitutes excellence; success and improvement against criteria; and pupils involved in deciding what and how they want to learn at initial planning stages and throughout a unit of work.

- **Reflectiveness**: all the evaluative reflective processes involved in formative assessment.

■ **Reciprocity**: talk partners and following ground rules for those; evaluating talking and listening and making improvements; talking and listening skill-building.

One teacher from the Moray Learning Team, Julie Oatridge, describes exactly how she uses Claxton's dispositions alongside principles of formative assessment:

Learning Muscles

The children in my class are used to working with learning intentions and success criteria, but I felt that some of their working habits needed to be improved. Having looked at Guy Claxton's learning dispositions and the four 'capacities' into which they are subdivided, I felt my class really needed to do work on **resilience**, particularly **managing distractions** and **absorption**. I spent ten minutes introducing Claxton's work to the children by using his analogy of going to the gym to work on muscles and strengthen them, and how it is the same with our learning muscles. By strengthening our learning muscles, it will help us to be better learners.

I showed them all the dispositions and the capacities, but said we would just focus on a few to start with. I have all these component parts of the four learning dispositions laminated on individual labels and colour-coded. **Managing distractions** was chosen first, as I felt some pupils were distracted easily. For 20 minutes with talk partners we discussed what distractions there were in the classroom: these were listed, and then we acted out how we could manage these distractions and the effectiveness of these strategies.

On our learning wall, where our learning intentions and success criteria are, we now have 'Our learning muscle is . . .' and then the 'managing distractions' laminated label. During the lesson I will remind the children that we are focusing on 'managing distractions' and ways that we can do that. I also give encouragement if I see a child managing a distraction well.

'Well done, I saw that Michael was trying to distract you, but you said you were busy and went back to your own learning.'

'Thank you, brain break manager, you could see we needed a break and engaged us in a brain gym activity to refocus us.'

Just as we talk about our learning intentions and success criteria, I just add in about the learning muscle we are working on. At the end of a lesson I ask the children on a scale of 1 to 10 (10 being brilliant) how effective they were at working at a particular muscle. The children then show me with their hands their score. I then ask a few children how it felt working this muscle. Responses show that they felt they were more focused on their work and more in control of their learning, and were pleased that they had used tactics to keep them on task.

After a week I introduced another capacity – **absorption**. Again we discussed the capacity with talk partners and came up with reasons why we needed to focus on this capacity. The label was added to our learning wall and was again mentioned in lessons, and encouragement was given when I saw children totally absorbed. We discussed how it felt to be totally absorbed and how the lesson just flew by when they were totally engrossed.

As each week goes by, I add another capacity. We are at the stage now where the capacities we have focused on are still on the learning wall under their disposition, and I now ask the children which particular muscle they are going to focus on to help with their learning. This is done at the beginning of each lesson. Some muscles relate more to some lessons than others, so they are the ones we specifically focus on. Children like the fact that they are in control of improving their learning, so instead of just being in class they are now working to become better learners. I also give examples of how, as an adult, I still have to use these muscles, and which ones I am working on.

Teachers and other educators

This book aims to help teachers see themselves as equal learners in every aspect of formative assessment. It seems incongruous to attempt to create the ideal learning environment for pupils if these principles are not also reflected in the learning environment for all adults working in the school. Andy Hind (2007) lists the following ingredients of 'an emotionally intelligent organisation':

Motivation of all individuals regularly monitored	Work/life balance encouraged and monitored	A culture of 'openness' and 'security'	Clear and agreed direction for future developments	Individuals demonstrate 'awareness' and 'responsibility' for development
Change handled effectively and welcomed by all	Clear and effective communication	Every member feeling valued and respected	Trust and challenge flow throughout	Shared and agreed values regarding core purpose

He describes change in three ways:

Shallow change impacts on policies, documents and resources.

Deep change impacts on skills and knowledge.

Profound change impacts on attitudes and behaviours.

This certainly resonates with the wealth of teacher feedback I have collated over the last ten years. Formative assessment strategies and techniques in place indicate only shallow change unless teachers' skills and knowledge are developed and, ultimately, they change or hone their attitude and behaviour regarding *the role of the pupil and the teacher*, so that active learning through formative assessment can flourish.

Letting go . . .

Control in the classroom features regularly in feedback discussions on Learning Team feedback days. For many teachers, getting pupils to generate success criteria which are then used by them to evaluate their work, and discussing questions asked with a talk partner, significantly changes the locus of control. Instead of the *teacher* doing most of the talking, and telling, it is the *pupils*. Having success criteria and being involved in the constant process of analysis – whether of previous pupils' work or reviewing existing work – means there is a continual handover from teacher to pupil. One secondary teacher from the Birmingham Learning Team described his development, after one term of introducing success criteria and talk partners, as follows:

'The whole process has helped me learn that I am still becoming a teacher. I started off teaching by just surviving and making sure that I was totally in control. Now, nine years down the road, I have for the first time realised that I can give some of that control to the students. I am now letting them in on the secret and letting go of my own insecurities in my teaching.'

Reflection

- Do you have a fixed mindset (an entity learner) or a growth mindset (an incremental learner)?
- What about your pupils?
- Can you think of what might have made you develop either a fixed or growth mindset from your past: e.g. the phrasing of praise or encouragement, or the message that ability was fixed for good, or that you were 'intelligent'?
- Do you think that external rewards really work in making pupils effective self-motivated learners?
- How much say do your pupils have in determining the ideal learning environment?
- Which of Claxton's four learning dispositions are most in need of attention in your class/es or school?
- How far have you let pupils have control of the learning in your own classroom?

4 How can we maximise opportunities to think, discuss and question?

6 *If you have to talk, you have to think. I get to learn things from other people I didn't know.* 9

Five-year-old

Pupil talk is central to active learning. Establishing **talk partners** is often the first step teachers take in experimenting with formative assessment, as it is relatively straightforward to embark on and the impact can be seen immediately. This chapter explores talk partners in some depth, with many examples, as this has been the focus of my work within the subject of effective questioning. This chapter therefore deals with the place of talk in active learning, and the next gives examples of effective questioning templates for any subject or age group, with details of impact along the way.

The central role of 'dialogic' talk

The dominance of constructive, pupil 'dialogic' talk in a classroom is a key identifier of a 'formative assessment' culture, in which pupils are actively involved in thinking: effective pupil talk playing a central role in the philosophy of citizenship, personalisation and lifelong learning.

Many teachers report, on their first feedback session in learning teams, how the main change in their classroom is in who is doing the talking. Whereas traditional classrooms have an almost continual *teacher* voice – talking to the class or to individuals – when pupils have learning or talk partners, there is instead a constant handover to pupils when questions are asked and tasks are underway. Teachers have been doing too much work: pupils are now working harder because they are more motivated and in greater control. With the advent of talk partners, there is no longer any opportunity for pupils to opt out while the confident few do most of the talking and thinking. Teachers have more time to listen to pupils, noting the level of understanding and addressing any misconceptions on the spot, leading to more immediate feedback and modification of plans to meet learning needs as they arise: active learning and formative assessment in action.

A rationale for dialogic talk

Dialogic talk and *dialogic teaching* are terms Robin Alexander (2004) uses in his publication *Towards Dialogic Teaching*, in which he outlines the need for improving talk in the classroom and his various projects in England in which his ideas were investigated. His key points provide an effective rationale for the work many of us have been carrying out in finding ways to give all pupils a voice: a way to talk about their learning in what has been for them, until quite recently, a passive, mainly silent, teacher-controlled environment.

Alexander sets the scene:

❛ By the age of 4, the child of professional parents in the US will have had nearly twice as many words addressed to it as the working-class child, and over four times as many as a child on welfare. For the middle-class child, encouragement from parents vastly outweighs discouragement; but for the child on welfare the climate of adult reaction is an overwhelmingly discouraging one. While talk is essential for intellectual and social development, for some children the talk which they engage in at school is nothing less than a lifeline. ❜

He describes **dialogic teaching** as:

- **collective**: teachers and pupils address learning tasks together, whether as a group or as a class, rather than in isolation;

- **reciprocal**: teachers and pupils listen to each other, share ideas and consider alternative viewpoints;

- **supportive**: pupils articulate their ideas freely, without fear of embarrassment over wrong answers; and they help each other to reach common understandings;

- **cumulative**: teachers and pupils build on their own and each other's ideas and chain them into coherent lines of thinking and enquiry;

- **purposeful**: teachers plan and facilitate dialogic teaching with particular educational goals in view.

He states that the contexts and conditions for dialogic teaching are facilitated and supported when:

- teachers are prepared to change classroom layout to met the requirements of different kinds of learning tasks and different kinds of learning talk;

- lesson introductions and conclusions are long enough to make a difference, and, as far as possible, are concerned with ideas rather than procedures;

- *'Now let's talk about it'* becomes as familiar as *'Now let's write about it'*;

- teachers shift from interactions which are brief and random to those which are longer and more sustained;

- more and better use is made of oral assessment;

- teachers are sensitive to the way their expression, gesture, body language, physical stance and location in the classroom can affect the type and quality of classroom talk; teachers recognise that in all aspects of classroom talk they themselves are influential models.

Alexander explains that pupils' learning talk should consist of the ability to:

- narrate,
- explain,
- instruct,
- ask different kinds of question,
- receive, act and build upon answers,
- analyse and solve problems,
- speculate and imagine,
- explore and evaluate ideas,
- discuss, argue, reason and justify,
- negotiate,

and to do this effectively they need to:

- listen,
- be receptive to alternative viewpoints,
- think about what they hear,
- give others time to think.

One of the most exciting elements of teachers' action research is the impact they report after setting up talk partners in their classrooms. Much has been learnt in the teams about best ways of facilitating talk partners, not only organisationally, but also in extending the quality of pupil talk. All of Alexander's elements of pupils' talk arise through effective questions and talk partners, as trialled and developed by the learning teams.

As the majority of paired pupil discussions are the result of teachers' questions, time has also been devoted to the asking of effective questions – replacing recall questions with questions that promote thinking, discussion and the deepening of pupil understanding. As Alexander says, however:

> There's little point in framing a well conceived question and giving children ample "wait time" to answer it, if we fail to engage with the answer they give and hence with the understanding or misunderstanding which that answer reveals: we need to tell children not only what we think of their answers but why we think them and make it clear that our opinions are one of many.

We know that discussion and scaffolded dialogue have the greatest cognitive potential, but we have also found that these demand much of teachers' skill and subject knowledge. In order to engage effectively with pupils in worthwhile dialogue, we often need a very secure grasp of the subject of the lesson. **Decontextualising** learning objectives (*e.g.* 'to be able to cut along a line – context: making snowflakes' rather than 'to be able to make a snowflake'*) and identifying success criteria go a long way towards building subject expertise, because you need to know or find out what the learning objective actually consists of if you break it down.

The impact of talk partners and effective questioning is explored through teachers' feedback throughout this chapter and the next, but the key findings about **cognitive development** are that all pupils are involved in thinking and talking about their thinking, which has led to higher quality writing, a higher level of speaking and listening, and increased confidence in their ability to contribute and feel a sense of value as a class member. The **social impact** has also been significant, resulting in greater tolerance, support and empathy between pupils, regardless of gender, achievement level, race, religion or class.

What we have learnt so far to ensure quality talk in the classroom:

- Pupils need to have thinking time to answer a question, but discussing with a talk partner during that time or using mini whiteboards makes the thinking time more productive.
- Talk-partner discussions need to be very focused and not too long (e.g. *30 seconds to come up with one thing you can see in this writing*; *One minute to think of a good simile for a cat*; *Two minutes to decide what has gone wrong in this calculation*) to avoid pupils' losing momentum and going off-task.
- Teachers need to avoid asking for 'hands up' because the same few children are always first with their hands up and do most of the answering – and most of the class opt out of listening and thinking as a consequence.
- Randomly paired talk partners is the most effective organisational device (some techniques are given below), with partners changing either weekly or fortnightly. Pupils appreciate the fairness factor and get to appreciate the rich variety of social and learning experiences they encounter because of the frequent change.
- Strategies need to be put in place to ensure quality talk, such as sharing the rationale and surveying opinion regularly about the impact of talk partners from pupils' point of view; using ice-breaking activities when partners change; generating success criteria for good talk and good listening; using these to discuss how well pupil talk is developing; and finding ways for pupils to self- and peer-evaluate their paired talk.
- Teachers need to avoid asking too many closed recall questions and ask more worthwhile questions which will extend pupil understanding and begin lessons in a more productive way, also revealing misconceptions which can then be addressed.
- Responses to children's responses need to be sensitive and respectful to establish an ethos of confidence to give one's opinion, whether that is right or wrong.

Examples of practice and the impact of talk partners, from across the age range, now follow. The last section of this chapter then deals with the results of teachers' experimentation with effective questioning.

Examples of techniques and impact of talk partners

Nursery/Reception (3, 4 and 5 year olds)

Techniques

▸ Initially, children need lots of modelling and support with strategies such as '*Tell me what your partner said*', or tell children to be A and B: A speaks to B first, then B speaks to A, so that each child's speaking and listening is ensured. Listening skills need to be taught. Very focused short tasks are the best way of getting children to listen to each other (e.g. *Decide one word which describes this tiger*).

▸ Using lollysticks with children's names or matching cards (e.g. knife and fork), to find their partner works very well for random pairing.

▸ Many teachers find that ice-breaker activities are very effective in gelling the pairs when they first meet. Charlotte Smith, a teacher in Lincoln, uses the following ideas:

- Mrs Brown's shopping basket memory game or its many versions (e.g. *'I went to the zoo and I saw. . .'*).
- In the mirror, copy actions.
- What/Who am I? riddles (e.g. *'I am grey, have a long nose'*, etc).
- Just a minute: pupils have one minute or less to talk about a random subject/word.

▸ Changing partners weekly seems to work best, although in the nursery, pairs change all the time.

▸ Some schools have found the 'SEAL' (Social and Emotional Aspects of Learning) activities very useful – see the DCSF website under the PSHE or Primary Strategy section (www.standards.dcsf.gov.uk).

▸ Teachers felt it was very important to explain the rationale of talk partners, including the random selection and the time change, so that children understand the fairness issue.

Impact
Cognitive development

■ Talk partners make children think more clearly about what they are doing and children write more as a consequence of talking more.

■ Increased cooperation has led to more unprompted peer support (e.g. children are seen whispering prompts to each other: *'Amazing for this age group!'*)

■ One teacher found that having talk-partner success criteria had led to children being able to develop debating skills (e.g. *'I disagree with you because. . ..'*)

■ Teachers are made more aware of children's misconceptions or ways of seeing the world (e.g. one child to another *'Where does the moon come from?'*, *'It comes out of the earth's tummy.'*)

- One child with limited English has been able to report back as a direct result of the support he received from his talk partner: *'It was amazing what he had picked up.'*

- A non-speaking child from a pre-school setting had learnt, through talk partners, to talk and share.

- One teacher was concerned at how the increased noise level had disturbed a child with Asperger's Syndrome. In other teams, children with Asperger's Syndrome had become used to the new set-up and had benefited by changing partners regularly and being encouraged to discuss with their partner.

Social development

- Children are more tolerant and accepting of one another, and respect between children is increased.

- One child with very challenging behaviour became kind and considerate when paired with a girl, but annoying when paired with another boy. The class stopped the lesson to talk about his bad behaviour, as the teacher now allows them to express their opinion about things, which she never did before. The impact of the peer disapproval led to a complete change in his behaviour.

- Children are forming new friendships and wanting to go to their new friends' houses, which has changed their mums' friendship groups!

- On the playground, if they have arguments, they can actually step back and talk about and resolve it, rather than kicking and punching, as cooperation and respect formed through talk partners carries over to other situations.

Years 1 and 2 (6 and 7 year olds)

Techniques

▶ Modelling good/bad talk partners and drawing up success criteria is a necessary and very effective element.

▶ Sharing the rationale for talk partners with both children and parents is vital, to prevent complaints about random partnering.

▶ One teacher uses an amber pot and a green pot for answering questions. Lollysticks with children's names on are moved from the amber pot to the green pot when a question has been answered. They are also used to choose who will answer a question. It is important that this technique is used *after* talk-partner discussions, so there is time for every child to have a considered response.

▸ Gillie van der Eyken, a teacher in Dorset, creates a display board for current talk partners. She photographs each child and places Velcro on the back of each photo. The photos are put into a box and drawn out randomly and placed in pairs on the display board. This is very useful for reminding children who their partner is and is a useful tool for visitors to the classroom. Children then have a *'meeting moment'* every Monday morning, where they first say goodbye to their old partner by shaking their hand and saying something positive. They then go to sit with their new partner and have an ice-breaker activity, such as taking turns to copy a facial expression, drawing an alien together, building a Lego tower or some other practical activity. The children look forward to their weekly change of partner. This system is now in place across the school.

Some typical comments:

Reception: *'I like it when I sit with my talk partner because then I listen better and don't get fidgets in my bottom.'*
Year 1: *'My learning partner is very good at listening to me and always says my work is cool.'*
Year 2: *'I really like it when we can start off with our talk partner because we can share ideas.'*
Year 4: *'When we do something with a learning partner it is good because you get double the ideas and your work is doubly better!'*
Year 6: *'I think it is good when we can cooperate with anyone, then people don't just want to work with their best friend all the time and you can work with people you might not normally work with.'*

Impact – *as above, plus:*
Cognitive development

■ All children now have answers and feel no pressure because they are part of a paired response and there is time to discuss.

■ Children are learning and teaching when they are in talk partners, so all pairings gain.

■ There is greater pupil engagement and less passive listening.

■ Children are more confident speakers, explaining and paraphrasing, using more extensive vocabulary and have better listening skills.

■ Teachers are realising that some children's responses reveal they are at a higher level than the teacher had previously given them credit for.

- Teachers have more time with children, and their role is now listening and picking up on achievements and misconceptions. Teachers are talking less and children talking more, discussing and giving input.

- More activities now seem to be oral rather than written.

- Pupils with language delay are able to listen better with a talk partner and one child with Kabuki Syndrome (limited language and other skills) who did not really speak, via talk partners has learnt to interact and is now more accepted by the class.

- In one East Lothian school, a fire officer was invited to the school to talk to the Primary 2 and 3 classes as part of the 'People who help us' topic. The officer asked *'Who can tell me what we could do to make our homes safer?'* One child put up her hand and asked *'Can we do talk partners?'* The teacher explained the system to him, a child set off the one-minute timer and pairs began discussing the question. The officer was most impressed by the purposeful discussion and how well they answered after it. Children had taken ownership of the whole situation.

- In one school, teachers were convinced that the increase in the higher levels gained through testing was a direct result of talk partners. A section of the display from their Essex Learning Team showcase day can be seen in Fig. 4.1, in which the scores are explained.

Social development

- The gender gap has closed. One boy used to refer to all girls as 'her', but now uses their names.

- Personality clashes are not the issues teachers expected. Because children see the fairness of the random pairing, and their discussions are so focused, they don't have time to misbehave or talk about things that don't really matter. They do not want to let each other down.

- Any problems with pairings (for a very few children in some classes in the first few weeks) tend to be caused by boys. Once children have had several pairings, they look forward to the change.

- Children know each other better, so bullying is less of an issue. For example, one child said at first *'She's a swot. I'm not going to work with her.'* At the end of the three weeks she said *'Emma was great to work with because she really listens to you.'*

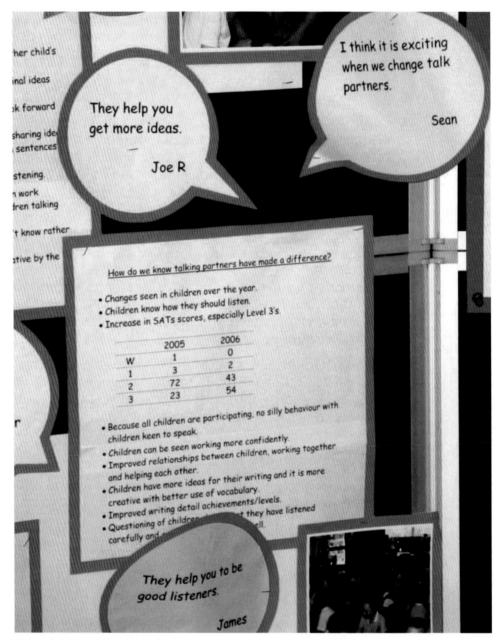

Fig. 4.1 The impact of talk partners in raising attainment

Years 3 and 4 (8 and 9 year olds)

Techniques

▸ One teacher from the Blackburn with Darwen Learning Team
  introduced a self- and partner evaluation sheet for children to
  complete at the end of the two weeks, before they changed to a new

partner (see Fig. 4.2) using class success criteria. They complete one side of the form to evaluate themselves and the other side to evaluate their partner. Pairs then swap sheets and have a frank (yet polite!) discussion about each other's comments. The teacher discussed this in great detail, talking about the importance of them expressing their opinions, agreeing or disagreeing and giving reasons. The technique has been very successful and has led to children focusing on how they could improve their talking and listening skills.

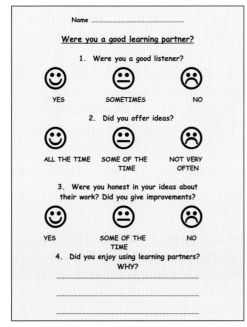
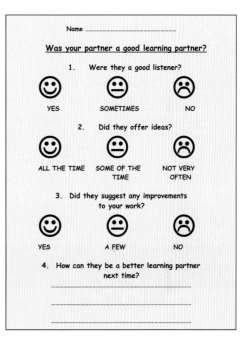

Fig. 4.2 Self-evaluation form

▸ Helen Rowley and Tracey Wheeler, from the Birmingham Learning Team, created 'compliment slips' for children to complete before they change partners. They are written for their partner and given to them as they part company. Examples can be seen in Fig. 4.3. These teachers found them very effective and popular with the

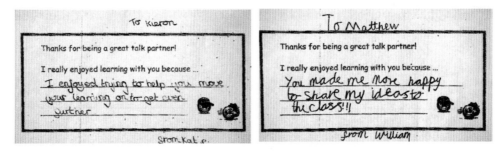

Fig. 4.3 Compliment slips

children. Helen also describes the class-based research she conducted about talk partners in the 'Impact' section below.

▸ Sharing the rationale with children and parents is vital. Children can be sulky at first if they are not clear about how the system will work and its purpose. The fairness principle is very important to children. Some will even check the system (e.g. one teacher has cards with children's names on, which she shuffles, but the class insists that one child each time verifies the shuffling!)

▸ Moira Bearwish, from the Dorset Learning Team, introduced talk partners for the start of the new academic year with a Year 4 class by fully involving parents and setting expectations:

At the end of summer term the Year 4 team spent some time with their new class, still Year 3. We introduced the idea of talk partners, what they were, how we saw them working and their purpose. Each teacher decided a way of organising the partners. We each wrote the children's names on a card to be kept in our treasure boxes. Children chose the upside-down cards at random for their talk partner.

A letter accompanied children home to explain talk partners. We asked for parental support.

The children's task over the summer was to send their partner a postcard which was addressed to the school.

The first two weeks' learning in Year 4 was planned around speaking and listening. Success criteria were identified for talkers and listeners, and visual prompts were made. Partners' first task was to discuss their postcards, ask each other questions and feed back to the whole group. Pairs change every two weeks through random picking of names.

▸ It is important for visitors to the school to be aware of the 'no hands up' talk-partners policy. or children can be thrown by unexplained, different expectations.

▸ It is very successful to place a child with English as an additional language in a two, making a three.

▸ Teachers have control over which pairs sit where. This can be useful, as some teachers have found if good friends are sitting next to each other, they are tempted to talk together rather than with their talk partner.

▶ Two teachers at a 4–19 Birmingham special school for pupils with moderate learning difficulties made the following points about talk partners with their own pupils:

- *Explaining and modelling talk partners was given much time at the beginning.*
- *Random partners was not successful with certain personalities.*
- *Success criteria were displayed at all times.*
- *Practical physical prompts – such as a bell to start/stop talking and an egg timer as a visual aid – were very successful.*
- *Thinking time extension was necessary for children to process information (e.g. children with autistic spectrum disorder require at least eight seconds to assimilate and interpret language.)*
- *Using 'no hands up' and getting pairs to respond is useful for pupils with special needs, as it encourages them to work collaboratively. It can remove feelings of being overwhelmed with the task of coming up with an individual response.*
- *An elective mute pupil was effectively given a voice via talk partners when careful partnering was used for her.*

Impact: *a positive impact on behaviour; children are engaged and enjoy lessons; pupils are taking a more active part in lessons; the physical, practical talk has made them less passive learners.*
Learning, *as a consequence, became more enjoyable and less of a situation in which to fail. For many pupils in special schools, this is exactly what their experience had been at their former schools.*

Impact – *as above, plus:*
Cognitive development

■ Children give more detailed answers: they are gradually developing higher-quality talk.

■ They are clearly processing their thoughts and rehearse them before saying them out loud, resulting in a faster pace for many classes.

■ Self-esteem has been boosted, especially for lower achievers.

■ Teachers have more time to listen and interact with children.

■ Talk partners are good for a composite class (small classes of mixed ages, usually in rural areas), as younger children became more confident and are better able to discuss with older children.

■ Knowing that there will be a change in two or three weeks keeps learning fresh. Children get very excited at the thought of a new partner.

■ In one class, a high-achieving Year 4 pupil was paired with a Year 3 pupil. The higher achiever blossomed as a natural teacher and spent lots of time explaining things to the other child. This had benefited both children enormously – bringing a great confidence boost for the higher achiever and effective learning for the younger pupil. The teacher said *'It was incredible watching them.'*

■ On a school trip, several schools were on site and a quiz was organised. A question was thrown out to see who could answer the quickest: one school put up their hands immediately, so gained the points. Children from this teacher's school immediately broke into talk partners to discuss the question, so lost the points! Children need to know the *purpose* of a question, as the required quick response was clearly not indicated.

■ Helen Rowley, with her class of mixed Year 3 and 4, organised random partners with 'no hands up' and allowed between 5 and 30 seconds to talk with their partner. Towards the end of their first three weeks with their first partner, in April, six children were interviewed about their views. Helen then focused on helping children to give responses as a pair rather than as individuals, (e.g. elaborating on the initial response or helping out if a partner was stuck). After three months, she interviewed the same children again. The children's views indicated significant development in their ability to think about themselves as learners. William's first and second responses are shown below:

William's April interview (partnered with Sian)
1. *It's a really fair way to choose, because we will all get to work with different people and that's good, because people have different ideas.*
2. *Perhaps it would be better to have your partner for a shorter time than three weeks, so that you could get more partners – I don't think we'll get time for many.*
3. *Having a partner is good because it makes you feel more confident – me and Sian were already confident, but now I am better at sharing my ideas and listening to Sian.*

William's July interview (partners have included Sian, Josh, Ruby and Matthew)
1. *Having a learning partner helps you to be more confident to talk to the class.*
2. *Since I have had a learning partner I have tried to share my ideas more.*
3. *Josh is helping me to put my ideas into words that make more sense – like explaining the strategy, not just saying the answer.*
4. *Having random partners is a good way to choose because it's fair and there are no squabbles or blame.*
5. *Girls used to be the last resort for a partner, but it's better now because you get more ideas.*
6. *I can't think of anything that's not good about having learning partners.*

7. *When people used to put their hands up it was annoying and it put people off answering, and also people who know the answer sometimes don't bother to put their hands up anyway;*
8. *We don't have 'sitting up straight' now either; Mrs Rowley just asks anybody, because everybody's talked about it. Sitting up can put people off too.*

Social development

■ Many teachers report that – to their amazement – disruptive children, randomly paired, tend to work well and become better behaved.

Years 5 and 6 (10 and 11 year olds)

Techniques

▸ Basic techniques described in previous year groups of random pairings, 'no hands up', etc, were used with this age group.

▸ The point was made in several teams that pupils of this age can be rather 'hormonal' and react in a particular way if pairings are publicly announced (!) While this technique works well with younger children, it seems more tactful to, say, let pupils pick a face-down card which tells them their new partner.

▸ One teacher had spent a lot of time with this age group talking about the rationale for talk partners, and also how they might feel if they were paired with someone they were not happy to be with and how they might cope with that. This proved to be very worthwhile. A school inspector commented on how well the pupils were working together and assumed that they were all in friendship groups, even though they were in fact randomly paired.

▸ One teacher found it useful to have 'quality checks' against talk-partner success criteria by giving out prompt cards (e.g. *'What would you do if your friend was caught shoplifting?'*) and then analysing how effective their speaking and listening had been after a three-minute discussion between talk partners.

▸ There is great potential for team building and using the pairs together (e.g. pairs into fours to solve a problem).

Impact – *as above, plus:*
Cognitive development

■ There are higher quality discussions and pupils often rethink answers and realise that there is often more than one solution or opinion.

- Pupils are kept on-task. One pupil said *'It makes my brain work better.'*

- Pupils understand and appreciate the value of talk partners. One pair, told they would lose the privilege of working as a pair because they were off-task, begged for this not to happen. Pupils now expect that talk will be a big part of a lesson. Pupils find peer support very valuable. A typical comment from a pupil: *'If I get stuck, I'd ask my partner rather than the teacher.'*

- Evaluations reveal that pupils become very skilled at assessing their own and their partner's talk (e.g. *'Don't be afraid to say I've done something badly.'*)

- Low achievers have opportunities to shine orally, which has boosted their confidence. Many teachers believe that *lower* achievers benefit the most from talk partners – but there are as many teachers who say that the coaching and explanation skills benefit *higher* achievers the most.

- Not working in ability groups helped the progress of pupils with special needs in particular. An elective mute is now able to share her ideas, as a result of talk partners.

- The teacher's role is more that of a guide than a leader. More teaching and less controlling is taking place. Teachers are making better assessments.

- 'No hands up' led to more contributions from girls.

- One school had a week where pupils designed how they would be taught. They did not have talk partners and the classroom reverted to only a few pupils asking questions. Many pupils opted out, as they were not involved and said that lessons were boring. This brought home to the teachers and pupils how vital talk partners really are.

Social development

- New friendships flourish as pupils are paired with children they would not have wanted/dared to have talked to before.

- Lower achievers have to talk things through, which has helped develop their emotional intelligence.

- One teacher deliberately chose four difficult boys to work together and found that they were better behaved than they would have been if sitting apart.

- One pupil with autism who is usually isolated socially was paired with a chatty boy. Both initially spoke to the teacher and not to each other. After ten minutes they had moved physically closer and were talking to each other.

Secondary (12–18 year olds)

Techniques

▸ Random partners need to be thoroughly discussed, as there can be initial resistance with students beginning this late in their education. However, most of the feedback about random pairings is very positive.

▸ Because teachers often only meet a class once a week, the pairings might need to last longer than two weeks.

▸ One school put names on desks or mixed-up exercise books, randomly placed.

▸ Use of mini whiteboards has been invaluable for students privately first jotting their ideas.

▸ In one secondary school there was great reluctance by students to be paired randomly, and the teachers had given up after two weeks. In two other secondary schools, they persisted, confronting students' prejudices and explaining the rationale and possible feelings in depth. Students had greatly benefited as barriers were broken down and both cognitive and social impact took place.

▸ In one 4–19 special school, it was a slow process to use talk partners, especially with pupils who were autistic and found it difficult to work with others. One teacher said it took five months for those pupils to reap the rewards. One pupil articulated to the teacher that she was glad she had been made to work with different talk partners because she could now work with anyone and previously had been hiding in her shell.

▸ In the same special school, the impact from one class was felt throughout the school. A deaf child signed to her partner that she felt there should be more pupils taught to sign in school so more people could understand her and communicate with her. Before talk partners, her voice would not have been heard. In this school many pupils have poor communication skills and sensory problems and they rely on staff to help them communicate. The school is now, as a result of this request, putting measures in place to have more pupils learning to sign.

Impact
Cognitive and social development

■ Lower achievers have now been brought into the learning arena.

- Communication skills have developed tremendously, between students and students and students and teachers.

- Teachers could tell if students were having difficulties because they talked much less.

- Teachers had previously underestimated the cognitive or social strengths of some of the students.

- By raising the status of talk (*'Talking is another way to learn'*) there was less off-task chatter. There had been a huge impact on self-esteem and confidence because students' views were seen to count.

- One teacher asked students to come up with a graph about rainfall and temperature and say why they had chosen, say, a line graph to show temperature. Their answers were exemplary – probably, the teacher thought, because they were not being spoonfed, did not feel threatened and had time to discuss the task.

- Pupils became more accountable, more willing to attempt tasks.

- Quotes from students: *'It helped me understand things more when you come to an agreement'*, *'Talk partners work well because you share ideas and compromise'*, *'They develop our friendships'*.

- In one school, teachers said students used to be reluctant to give answers for fear of failure, but feedback is now all-inclusive, with no pressure on any one student.

Reflection

- Are learning partners established in your classroom/school?
- Have you tried random partnering? If not, could pupil tolerances and social skills be improved by pupils working with anyone in the class?
- How difficult is it to get out of the 'hands up' habit?
- Have you asked pupils their opinion about talk partners and hands up?
- Could you involve pupils more effectively in saying what would help them learn better or how various classroom techniques could be improved?
- Which ways do you find best of informing parents about new things, such as talk partners?
- How far are existing talk partners truly engaged in quality talk, with both pupils equally involved?

5 Asking worthwhile questions

6 I like it when we have a question like this, as it does make me think and you have to explain it. It is really challenging! 9

Ten-year-old

Having talk partners, eliminating 'hands up' and giving pupils thinking time transforms a classroom, but the **kinds of questions** teachers ask determine how far the discussions will go in deepening and furthering children's learning and understanding. *Recall* questions dominate classrooms, mainly as a matter of habit. These are 'closed' questions, asked to assess whether pupils have learnt what they have been taught, to establish prior knowledge before teaching or to tune them back to something that was left in progress. Examples: *What are the two things we learnt about evaporation last week? What is 5 squared? What do plants need to grow? How did the story end?* These questions are more valid, of course, if there follows a minute or two of talk-partner discussion before responding. Recall questions have little value for assessment purposes because, unless every child is asked the same question, one child's answer is clearly unreliable as a class indicator. Using recall questions to tune pupils back can result in a confused pupil response, whereas a simple reminder from the teacher about the current focus is more straightforward and avoids the need for recall. We need to be asking pupils more questions which will extend their thinking and learning, and that has always been a challenging task.

My last book, *Formative Assessment in Action: weaving the elements together,* included a lengthy chapter on effective questioning, including De Bono's thinking hats, examples of Bloom's Taxonomy in questions about texts, 'Speaking, Listening and Learning' examples (DfES publication) and examples of children's questions. These are not repeated here although they are, of course, still relevant and useful.

Effective questions can be discussed under many educational headings – e.g. *formative assessment, thinking hats, thinking skills, philosophy for children.* 'Philosophy for Children', an approach to learning by Matthew Lipman (2003), was adopted by Robert Fisher (1996) in his *Stories for Thinking,* providing an interesting starting point for effective questions which come from pupils to create a 'community of enquiry' in the classroom (see www.sapere.org.uk). In a typical *Stories for Thinking* lesson, the teacher shares a 'thinking story' with the class. They have thinking time when they are asked to think about anything in the story that they consider was strange, interesting or puzzling. Their comments and questions are sought and each child's question is written up. The children then choose from the list which question they would like to discuss. Children discuss, giving reasons for their comments.

Over the last three years, teachers in the learning teams have experimented with other starting points for effective discussion in the classroom, especially focusing on five generic templates for questioning which were originally derived from analysing effective questions. These question templates have been extensively trialled and have proved very effective in creating a thinking classroom and in helping teachers become more aware of the impact of their questions. Most teachers from the teams find this one of the more challenging aspects of formative assessment, and come to it usually half-way through the year. However, teachers end the project by saying they now plan at least one worthwhile question per lesson as a result of seeing the impact on pupils' thinking. The questions are used in different ways: sometimes at the beginning of a lesson to tune children in and reveal their level of understanding (e.g. Statement: *Plants grow if you give them other liquids but not water. Do you agree or disagree?*), sometimes at the beginning of a unit or week to begin an investigation or research (e.g. Range of answers: *Why did Henry VIII have six wives?* He got fed up with them/He wanted a son and heir/He was pressured to produce a son by other people, etc).

The following pages give many examples of the five question templates, with some of the pupils' answers where I was able to procure them. Teachers ask me all the time for more examples of techniques in action, so my aim is that, by seeing as many examples as possible, teachers will feel empowered to use them as a starting point, then create their own. The examples given are almost all suitable to be presented to any age group, because they can be answered and thought about at all levels. Rather than attribute individual questions to individual teachers, they are all acknowledged at the end of this chapter.

Five templates for effective questions

1. A range of answers

2. A statement

3. Right and wrong

4. Starting from the answer or end

5. An opposing standpoint

1. A range of answers

> **Impact:**
> • develops thinking skills
> • improves reasoning skills
> • promotes discussion and explanation
> • reveals misconceptions
> • encourages debate

Ask a question and give a range of possible answers for children to discuss. Include definite *Yes* answers, definite *No* answers and some ambiguous answers to enrich the discussion. This template is not helpful when only one answer is correct and the rest are wrong, because there is very little to discuss!

Examples

1 A teacher from the East Lothian team asked pupils: **What do we need for life?**, and offered the answers: **water, telephones, clothing, cars, shelter, food**.

> **Some pupils' responses**
> *'You need cars to get to the hospital because if you walked, you'd be dead before you got there.'*
> *'You can't keep cars because they give out gases which go into your lungs and make it difficult to breathe which can kill you.'*
> *'If you have cars their fumes cause global warming which will melt the ice caps. The sea will rise and flood Scotland. People will drown and so cars will kill people.'*

2 One teacher, when working on air resistance, usually asks *'Who can remember what a streamlined shape looked like?'* This time she drew five different shapes on the board and asked them to discuss which shapes were streamlined. This produced high-quality discussion.

3   Another teacher read a poem to her Year 2 class, omitting the title (*The Train Ride*). Instead of only asking *'**What is the setting for this poem?**'*, she included a range of answers: **bus, train, bike, car, plane, boat**

> **Some children's responses:**
> *'It couldn't be a plane because it goes through a tunnel.'*
> *'It has to be a train.'*
> *'No, a car or a bike could go through a tunnel.'*

4   Dylan Wiliam (2006) gives an example of 'a range of answers' used in a secondary school, with some interesting variations:

> ***'What can we do to preserve the ozone layer?'***
> **A** *Reduce the amount of carbon dioxide produced by cars and factories.*
> **B** *Reduce the greenhouse effect.*
> **C** *Stop cutting down the rainforests.*
> **D** *Limit the number of cars that can be used when the level of ozone is high.*
> **E** *Properly dispose of air-conditioners and fridges.*

He describes a teacher who then asks the students to hold up one, two, three, four or five fingers depending on whether they think the answer is A, B, C, D or E. From this, she knows whether the students have learnt or need more teaching. Another teacher gets the students to group with others who have the same answer: they go to a corner of the room and they plan together how they are going to persuade the students in the other corners that they are wrong (the correct answer is E, because it is a question about the ozone layer, not global warming).

Further examples of a 'range of answers'

Are these foodstuffs good for you?
Chocolate, fruit, milk, meat, fat, sugar, salt, water, butter, margarine, rice pudding, motor oil, black pudding.

Which words are verbs?
Door, run, climb, comb, red, slide, spill, cycle, shout.

Which things are needed to plan a route?
Compass, watch, map, GPS, trundle wheel, car, flag, atlas, globe.

Which of these do you need to enjoy a successful lesson?
Listening, manners, drink, pencil, book, determination, patience.

Which of these language features would you need to use if you were going to write a diary entry?
Formal language, past tense, abbreviations, technical language, named people, present tense, informal language.

What makes a good school council member?
A good reader, a chatter box, a clear speaker, a good listener, a good writer.

When something unexpected happens, how do you feel?
Proud, worried, aggressive, anxious, jealous, happy.

Or as a variation . . .
Ask the *pupils* to come up with the range of answers (e.g. *The wolf disguised himself as grandma because . . .*). Ask for *right, wrong* and *could be* answers.

2. A statement

> **Impact:**
> • Encourages open discussion and debate
> • Develops critical thinking
> • Reveals misconceptions and understanding
> • Gives pupils confidence in expressing their opinions

Simply turn a question into a statement, and ask whether pupils agree or disagree with the statement, and to give reasons. 'Closed' questions, with one right answer, are clearly not as effective as those which need explanation.

Examples

1   Instead of asking *'What did a Viking look like?'*, one teacher said: **'This picture shows a Viking. Do you agree or disagree?'**

> **Some children's responses:**
> **Agree**
> *'He is a Viking because his badge has a Viking sign on it.'*
> *'He is wearing a cape.'*
> *'We think that he is a Viking because he has a scruffy beard.'*
>
> **Disagree**
> *'He is not wearing a helmet. All Vikings wore helmets.'*
> *'He doesn't have a sporran.'*
> *'The man has the wrong sword.'*

2 One teacher gave the statement: *'Batteries go flat'*.

Discussion revealed that some pupils thought that batteries went flat, in terms of depth. Some pupils insisted that they could flatten a battery, so they mind-mapped what a battery going flat means. Some pupils even took a hammer to a battery, but eventually understood that the batteries would not physically go flat!

3 A Year 10 English teacher asked: *'Money brings you happiness. Agree or disagree?'*

They then looked at a poem about status, equality and democracy in America, and students had to use evidence from the poem to support what they had said.

4 A primary teacher asked: *'Glass is an excellent material for making a shelter. Agree or disagree?'*

> **Pupil's response:**
> 'Both, because it's great for something waterproof and it lets warmth through. This is great for a greenhouse. But the glass can break easily because kids go throwing and batting balls and footballs while playing games but it can be secured by wood and poles. It's a great insulator because it keeps the warmth in but blocks the cold out.'

5 A high school teacher used a variation on the 'statement' template, asking instead of *'Do you agree or disagree?'*: *'Is this statement always, sometimes or never true?*

- **Multiples of 3 are always odd numbers.**

- **Odd numbers multiplied by even numbers have odd answers.**

6 One teacher used a statement as a starting point for a staff training day: *'Do not make children aware of a learning difficulty as it will damage their self-esteem.'*

This was very useful for stimulating discussion.

Further examples of 'a statement' questions

- Wood is a good material for making umbrellas because it is waterproof. Do you agree or disagree?

- Plastic toys are better than metal toys. Agree or disagree?

- Victorian children must have been very unhappy. Agree or disagree?

- Two opposite sides of a dice add up to 8. Agree or disagree?

- The moon is a source of light. Agree or disagree?

- Guy Fawkes was a bad man. Agree or disagree?

- Every school should have its own swimming pool. Agree or disagree?

- Pupils should be able to choose if they come to school. Agree or disagree?

- All pupils should learn a foreign language. Agree or disagree?

- Puberty is harder for girls than boys. Agree or disagree?

- Shylock was not a villain but a victim. Agree or disagree?

- Drugs in sports are morally wrong. Agree or disagree?

- All animals are predators. Agree or disagree?

- Everything is alive. Agree or disagree?

3. Right and wrong

> **Impact:**
> - Encourages problem solving
> - Identifies the success criteria
> - Stimulates curiosity and interest
> - Assesses knowledge
> - Reinforces previous learning
> - Demands explanation

Two opposites are presented to pupils. They are told that one is 'right' and one 'wrong', and they have to decide how we know this to be true.

An example

Instead of asking 'What would you find in a healthy meal?', show two pictures of meals and ask: **'Why is this meal healthy and this one unhealthy?'**

Responses from pupils:
'That meal is healthy because it has fruit and vegetables and we need to eat them to be healthy.'
'The other plate is all yellows and shows that the food has been cooked in fat and that is not healthy.'

Further examples of 'right and wrong' questions

- Why does this toy move and this one not?

- Why are these shapes quadrilaterals and these not?

- Why is a dandelion a weed when a daffodil is not?

- Why is this child happy and this child sad? (show two pictures, of a child sharing and a child not sharing)

- Why is this serve good and this one keep ballooning into the air? (tennis video)

- Why is this calculation right and this one wrong?

$$8 \div 0.5 = 16 \qquad 8 \times 0.5 = 16$$

4. Starting from the answer/end

Impact:
- Promotes reasoning skills
- Elicits prior knowledge
- Reinforces and revisits learning objectives
- Children identify the success criteria
- Good for assessment
- Inclusive, because all can come up with their own ideas and solutions, at many levels

This involves giving pupils the 'answer' or endpoint at the beginning and asking what they think the question might have been, how they think the answer might have been arrived at or *why* they think it is correct. This changes the focus from the answer itself to discussing *reasons* for the answer.

Examples of 'starting from the answer/end' questions

- Play fair is the answer. What might the question have been?

- Water, glass, the moon and shiny material can all do this. What might the question have been?

- The answer is square. What might the question have been?

- The answer is a map. What might the question have been?

- The answer is a list. What might the question have been?

- Here is my well-built house. What can you see?
- The Romans invaded Britain? Why?
- 1066 was a very turbulent year. Why?
- The prince kissed Sleeping Beauty and she woke up. What needs to be in place in the story before this happens?
- Bricks are the best material for building a house. Why?'

5. Opposing standpoint

This template involves introducing a different point of view in the question, rather than the conventional slant.

Impact:
- Improves debating skills
- Encourages reasoning skills
- Develops respect for other points of view
- Teachers get pupils to substantiate their opinions
- Encourages lateral thinking

Examples of 'opposing standpoint' questions

1 Instead of asking *'How did Cinderella feel about her stepmother?'*, ask: **'How could Cinderella have helped her stepmother become a better person?'**

> **Child's comment** (low achiever in writing – Level 2b):
> *'Cinderella didn't really think much about herself. She needed to stand up for herself. She just took it . . . the nonsense. Cinderella should have told her she was upset with her. The stepmother probably needed someone to stand up to her to stop her from being silly. She could have given her more friendship tokens or told her she loved her. Then the stepmother wouldn't have been jealous and liked her.*

2 One teacher asked, during a citizenship lesson, **'Is it fair that some children in the world do not have what we have?'**

The teacher gave a sweet to all the pupils wearing a watch. Other children were upset and the ensuing discussion led to children really understanding how it would feel to be treated unfairly, and that life is unfair and that some people treat others unfairly all the time.

3   One teacher asked: *'Should pupils be allowed on the grass every lunchtime?'*

Children's comments:
'No, the grass could be soaking and you might fall and hurt yourself.'
'Yes, because we would have more room in the playground. Little ones wouldn't get knocked over.'

Further examples of 'the opposing standpoint':

• How would a bully justify their actions?

• Why would some Celts think the Roman invasion was good?

• Would you buy a drug that has been tested on animals to cure a disease in a member of your family?

• Should school uniform be a matter of choice?

• Would it be OK to hit someone if you thought they were going to hit you?

• Should drugs be legalised?

• How do you think Louis Braille felt when the teachers at his school refused to use his invention?

• Should only girls be nurses?

• Should children who hurt each other not be punished?

• Should the mother do all the housework?

Children's final words

'I like it when we have a question like this as it does make me think and you have to explain it. It is really challenging!'
'I think that answering 'right or wrong' questions is good, because it helps us to think more and we are able to argue against one another.
'I think questions are good because they give us something to think about and give us time to think and I also like that we hear what other people think.'
'We get time to talk. The lazy people have to give an answer. It doesn't get boring for us.'

Teachers' responses to pupil responses

How teachers *respond* to pupils' answers is critical in determining the level of confidence pupils experience in feeling that they are able to say anything – a right answer, a wrong answer, a different opinion, a wondering question. The ethos of the classroom, whether teachers and pupils have a 'growth' or a 'fixed' mindset and how much say pupils have in their learning needs – all contribute to a learning environment in which pupils feel safe to speak and be treated with respect. Subtleties of body language, tone of voice and words need to be thought about carefully, so that 'put downs' do not occur in any form, which could stifle 'student voice'.

Leaving pupils with misconceptions does them a disservice and reinforces a fixed mindset, so misconceptions need to be dealt with in a 'grown-up' way, as if we were running a staff meeting. Effective strategies include:

Opening it up: Include the words *'do you think'* in any question (e.g. *How do you think an aeroplane stays up in the sky?*) so that a response becomes an opinion rather than a wrong answer.

Transfer: Say *'That was the answer to another question I was going to ask!'*

Gathering: *Does anyone agree? Disagree? Have a different opinion?*

Stalling: *I think you might want to come back to that idea a little later . . ..*

Returning to the same pupil: *Do you want to say something different now? I think I know where you were coming from before. You were put off/misled by the . . ..*

Reflection

- How many recall questions do you ask in a lesson? How effective are they in involving all pupils?
- How often are worthwhile questions planned for?
- Can you analyse questions you have asked which have generated high-quality thinking and discussion, and use the generic template for further questions in different contexts and subjects?
- Is there any way you could monitor the extent to which your body language, tone of voice and words used support or stifle pupil voice?

With thanks for the examples provided by:

Aaron Ackling, Woodhouse Primary School, Birmingham

Jen Allen, Geoffrey Field Infants and Nursery School, Reading

Natasha Allen, Welsh House Farm Primary School, Birmingham

Matthew Beresford, Stramongate Primary School, Cumbria:

Joanne Copestake from Woodhouse Primary School, Birmingham

Denbigh Community Primary School, North Tyneside

Angela Edmonds, Kings Norton Primary School, Birmingham

Melanie Fillier, Kings Norton Primary School, Birmingham

Ela McSorley, Four Dwellings High School, Birmingham

Lisa Naughton, Four Dwellings Primary School, Birmingham

Norham High School, North Tyneside

Tracey Wheeler, Nunnery Wood Primary School, Worcester

6 How can planning maximise pupil engagement and achievement?

6 *The way we're being taught now is like a weather forecast starting with the whole country and then going to the local area.* 9

16-year-old student

Over the last few years, teachers in the learning teams have focused on ways of making planning more meaningful and accessible to pupils. The original aim was to find ways of helping pupils see how today's lesson fitted the 'big picture' of the whole unit of work – to understand the rationale for its place and therefore to be more motivated and engaged. As teachers each year have built on previous strategies and techniques, this has developed considerably. A key feature is that pupils need to be fully involved at each stage. To summarise, this is what we have learnt so far:

To ensure maximum impact on motivation and achievement:

- Teachers/schools need to decide how they will make the curriculum more creative and flexible, focusing on key skills.
- Pupils need to be involved with the teacher in a pre-planning discussion for each unit of work to ensure appropriate pitch and to increase motivation and achievement.
- Pre-planning discussion needs to focus on what pupils already know, what they want to know (*knowledge*), what skills they want to learn (*processes*) and how they might go about learning those things (*the contexts*).
- Teachers need to present pupils with minimum coverage as a starting point for their discussions.
- The learning objectives, in the most accessible form, need to be displayed in some way so that there can be continual reference to where each lesson fits and where the learning is going.
- The display of learning needs to be interactive (e.g. showing what is already known, then gradually adding new learning to the display).
- There should be flexibility to change direction if pupil interest dictates it and it would not compromise necessary curriculum coverage.

The key issues of pre-planning and displaying learning interactively are now described in detail, and followed by examples across the phases of teachers' ideas in action and the impact these had on learning.

Pre-planning

(a) Moving to a key skills curriculum

Before any planning can be done, schools have to decide how they will cover the statutory curriculum. For some years, the most common approach in England was to follow the QCA (Qualifications and Curriculum Authority) schemes of work for each subject. These laid out specific learning objectives and activities, and were the result of teacher demand. Schools had been creating their *own* schemes of work, so there was a predictable outcry that it would be easier to produce national schemes. The QCA materials helped teachers see what progression through a subject would look like in practical terms, but after a while teachers felt over-constrained by the specificity of activities and contexts.

Following publication of *Excellence and Enjoyment* (DfES, 2003) and a general freeing-up of teacher demands, many schools have moved to a 'key skills' approach. There are various ways of approaching this, and the QCA materials are still often used, but more selectively. The main advantage of a key skills approach (found in the Programmes of Study and Literacy and Numeracy Frameworks) is that it greatly reduces the number of objectives and focuses planning on *process* rather then content. The context, or how the skills will be taught, is then free for schools and teachers to decide.

Having learnt about skills progression from the QCA materials, the best scenario would appear to be to focus on key skills, allow teachers and pupils to choose contexts (so the same unit might have the same title but be contextualised differently every year or have different activities) and bring together the best of the creative pre-National Curriculum practice with the rigour of today. This is not to say that the same context cannot be reused and that it is necessary to change – what is important is fitting the context to the cohort, in order to allow maximum access. External events might also be appropriate contexts at certain times (e.g. the Olympics). Resourcing does not need to be a problem if the same basic content is covered, but the approach is different.

One example of a key skills approach

Using the SEAL (Social and Emotional Aspects of Learning) key skills and various other sources, Jenny Short, School Development Advisor for Bath and NE Somerset Authority, produced, with teachers, the following list of non-subject-specific key skills:

- Enquiry
- Problem solving
- Social skills
- Managing feelings
- Evaluation

- Motivation
- Self-awareness
- Apply knowledge
- Creativity
- Empathy.

She then worked with teachers to produce lists of objectives for each year group for these skills, from Reception to Year 6 – these are shown in Fig. 6.1. (All of the examples shown in this section can be viewed in full at www.shirleyclarke-education.org.)

St Keyna Primary School, in the same local authority, then took these objectives and created 'I' statements so that they could be used by pupils (see Fig. 6.2), colour coding the key skills so that they could be tracked more easily through planning. After a year of trialling, the school is now about to refine the 'I' statements so that progression from year to year is more clearly defined. To date, this approach has been successfully used by both teachers and pupils.

Jenny Short also created medium- and short-term planning sheets in which the key skills feature (see Figs 6.3 and 6.4).

Subject-specific key skills

As well as *general* key skills, it seems that there also need to be *subject-specific* key skills, which are the tools pupils use to acquire knowledge. These key skills enable pupils to become lifelong learners, applying those skills in future contexts regardless of the content.

Fig. 6.5 shows both a literacy and history key skill and how the history skill might begin to be broken down into successive success criteria by children, via close analysis of old pieces of pupil work.

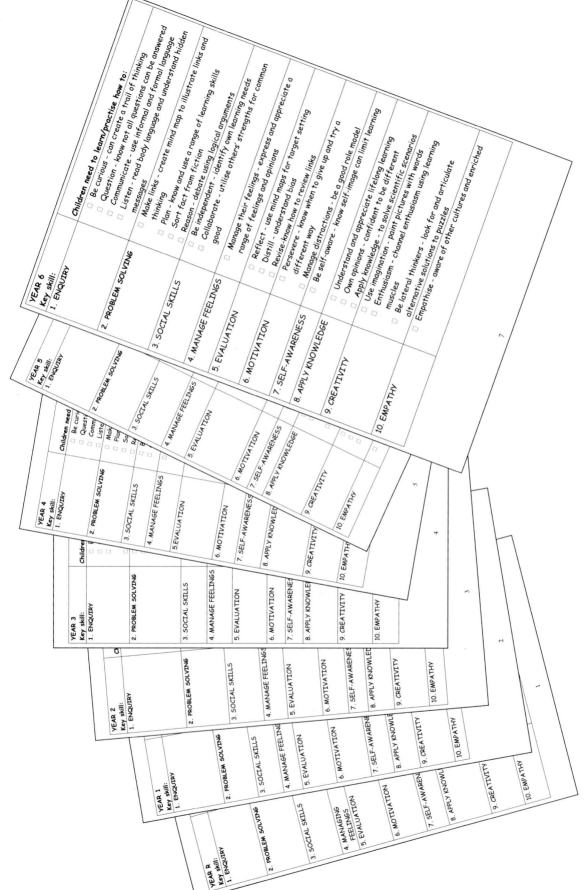

Fig. 6.1 Key Skills objectives, from Reception to Year 6 (with thanks to Jenny Short and Bath and North East Somerset Authority)

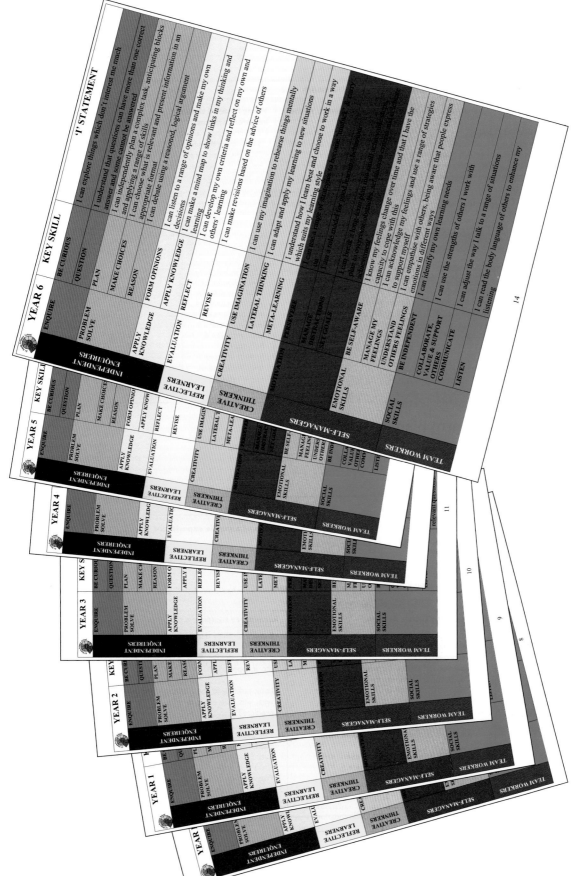

Fig. 6.2 'I' statements for key skills, from Reception to Year 6

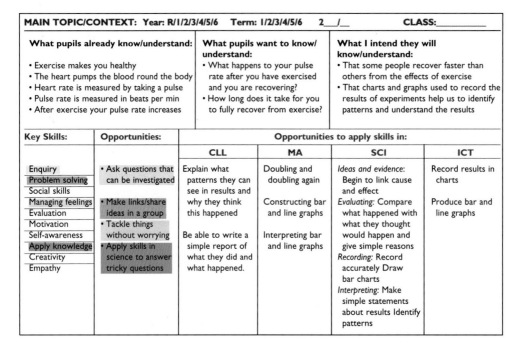

MAIN TOPIC/CONTEXT: Year: R/1/2/3/4/5/6   Term: 1/2/3/4/5/6   2__/__   **CLASS:**_____

What pupils already know/understand:	What pupils want to know/ understand:	What I intend they will know/understand:
• Exercise makes you healthy • The heart pumps the blood round the body • Heart rate is measured by taking a pulse • Pulse rate is measured in beats per min • After exercise your pulse rate increases	• What happens to your pulse rate after you have exercised and you are recovering? • How long does it take for you to fully recover from exercise?	• That some people recover faster than others from the effects of exercise • That charts and graphs used to record the results of experiments help us to identify patterns and understand the results

Key Skills:	Opportunities:	Opportunities to apply skills in:			
		CLL	**MA**	**SCI**	**ICT**
Enquiry Problem solving Social skills Managing feelings Evaluation Motivation Self-awareness Apply knowledge Creativity Empathy	• Ask questions that can be investigated • Make links/share ideas in a group • Tackle things without worrying • Apply skills in science to answer tricky questions	Explain what patterns they can see in results and why they think this happened Be able to write a simple report of what they did and what happened.	Doubling and doubling again Constructing bar and line graphs Interpreting bar and line graphs	*Ideas and evidence:* Begin to link cause and effect *Evaluating:* Compare what happened with what they thought would happen and give simple reasons *Recording:* Record accurately Draw bar charts *Interpreting:* Make simple statements about results Identify patterns	Record results in charts Produce bar and line graphs

Fig. 6.3 Medium-term planning for key skills

Key Skill	Learning Intentions	
ENQUIRY	**Curriculum LI: Record accurately and interpret results of a simple experiment**	
PROBLEM SOLVING	**Context: Investigating rate of recovery after exercise**	
SOCIAL SKILLS	**Key Skills LI: Listen to adults as well as children**	
MANAGE FEELINGS	**Make links and share ideas in a group**	
	Listen to and follow instructions	
EVALUATION	**Independent/Group Activity:**	**Remember to:** (*process success criteria*)
MOTIVATION	1. In groups of two, pupils find resting pulse rates then take turns to exercise for one minute and record pulse rate on a chart immediately after exercise and at 2-min intervals.	• Record carefully during the experiment. • Transfer the results to a graph/bar chart, etc, if appropriate.
SELF-AWARENESS	2. Pupils transfer their results to either a bar chart or a line graph or use the computer to construct same.	• Look carefully at the results and talk about what was different from what you had predicted.
APPLY KNOWLEDGE	3. **With support, pupils talk about their results, compare graphs, look for**	
CREATIVITY	**patterns and draw simple conclusions.**	• Talk about anything that surprised you. • Next, agree what you think you have found
EMPATHY	**PLENARY: Selected pupils present their findings and explain their thinking.**	out. • Together, write a sentence or two to explain what you discovered and your thinking
Assessment/notes to inform next steps:	Differentiation:	

Fig 6.4 Short-term planning for key skills

Subjects *(from National Curriculum)*	**History** **Literacy**
Context *(determined with pupils)*	**A diary entry for Henry VIII**
Key skills *(from History Programmes of Study/Literacy Framework)*	**1. Are the historical facts accurate?** **2. Is this how a Tudor would have phrased it?** **3. What are the features of diary writing?**
Broad success criteria for each skill *(identified by pupils via analysis of pupil finished work)* – one example shown	**1. <u>Are the historical facts accurate?</u>** • The facts are set in the right time • The events, people, etc, mentioned were real • There is evidence to support the historical facts
Further breakdown of success criteria *(identified by pupils via more specific analysis)* – one example shown	***<u>The facts are set in the right time</u>*** • *References to objects, food, transport, homes, clothing, etc, are as they would have been at that time* • *There are no references to anything modern or in a different historical period (e.g. watches, cars or caves)* • *Unsure facts have been checked for accuracy* • *Research has taken place before the diary was written*

Fig. 6.5 Subject-specific key skills

The purpose of illustrating these approaches is not to dictate, but to stimulate thinking and further ideas about a key skills curriculum.

(b) Pre-planning discussions with pupils

It is too late on the first day of a unit to ask pupils what they know and what they want to know, because the planning has already been done by the teacher. Teachers, therefore, need to meet with new classes in June or July for autumn-term planning.

Pre-planning discussions need to focus on what pupils already know, what they want to know *(knowledge)*, what skills they want to learn *(processes)* and how they might go about learning those things *(the contexts)*. A significant discovery by the learning teams was that simply giving pupils the title of the unit, or even broad headings, is not as effective as presenting them with the minimum coverage you need to adhere to and then asking *'What do you already know about these things?'* If you leave it too broad (*'What do you already know about the rainforest?'*), you get random thoughts and an incomplete picture. If, however, you give them a list of the objectives you want to explore about rainforests, and ask them – in talk partners – to decide how much they already know about those elements, you get a much more accurate picture of prior knowledge, with a clear idea of misconceptions. This, of course, impacts where a teacher pitches the learning and how much time they need to spend on it. Many teachers across the teams, having tried this, said that they realised how, in the past, they had either given pupils work which was beyond them or, more often, focused on things they had already done or already knew. Teachers often said that they had previously unwittingly missed opportunities to build on what pupils *already* know.

Similarly, asking pupils what they want to find out, given a blank canvas can result in two year's worth of ideas which have to be turned down for lack of time! If the minimum coverage is offered as the starting point, the question can then be asked *'What else would you like to find out?'* and the results are usually more feasible. This level of pupil involvement at the pre-planning stage leads to pupils coming up with ideas for contexts and activities, and obviously becoming more able to do this as they progress through the school.

Keeping the learning visual and interactive

In order to avoid the *'I wonder what this lesson will be about?'* syndrome, pupils need to be fully involved in the planning process, and be constantly aware of how the class learning is progressing, how today's lesson fits the whole unit and, especially, what learning is about to come. Some kind of display of learning objectives – whether on walls or flipcharts or inside pupil books – can be used to fulfil these aims, as long as they are moving and developing along with the learning itself. 'Working walls', 'learning walls' and a variety of inventive displays have been very successfully used for this purpose. For instance, one primary teacher had a large cut-out tree on one wall with the prior knowledge written on the roots, the questions to be explored on the trunk, and the new learning pasted up as leaves on the tree as time passed. The learning objectives found in the teacher's plan are usually inaccessible and are best rephrased as questions or abbreviated as aspects to be explored. It should not be a surprise to know that, when pupils are fully aware of what learning is to come, they are motivated, excited and interested. They research at home and come up with ideas for activities.

Examples of pupils' involvement in planning

Nursery/Reception (3, 4 and 5 year olds)

▸ In one school, children do mind maps on a Friday to find the starting point for their learning. At the end of the following week, they do another one to see how much they have learned.

▸ Taking children's initial ideas has resulted in more investigative learning (e.g. children carried water across the playground to see what it was like living in an African village).

▸ Unpicking children's responses in the initial discussion is useful (e.g. asked what they knew about light, one child said 'pasta'. Some pasta in the home had boiled dry and caught fire and the child thought the light had come from the pasta.).

In a Birmingham school, Lisa Killelay created 'before' and 'after' posters with the children to show what they had learnt about shapes (see Fig.6.6).

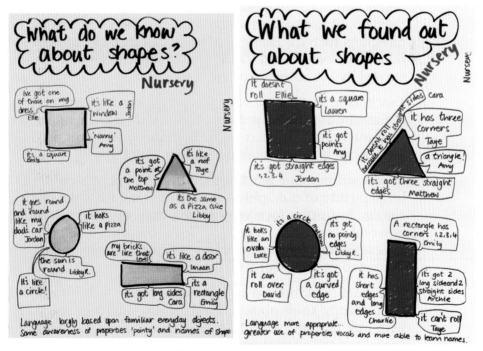

Fig. 6.6 Shape topic – 'before' and 'after' posters

Impact

- Children are more motivated and interested than before, especially boys.

- Children are learning at a higher level than previous foundation classes.

- Increased technical vocabulary.

- More parental involvement as the result of talk at home.

- Children are more engaged.

- More investigative learning.

- Time is saved, as covering things the children already know is avoided.

- Misconceptions can be dealt with more effectively as a result of children's comments at the pre-planning stage.

Years 1 and 2 (6 and 7 year olds)

▸ One teacher's pre-planning discussion revealed that children already knew what plants need to grow. She stopped them, gave a little input about plant growth to extend their knowledge and then asked what they would like to learn about plants. They came up with a list of questions such as *'Plants need water, but do they just need a drink or continuous water?'* and *'Do other kinds of drinks work?'* Children were very excited by the subsequent experiments.

▸ Teachers in one school were excited by the impact of giving children the minimum coverage as the basis of their discussions, realising that they rarely have to start at the beginning of a unit because prior knowledge is much more accurately defined.

▸ Report writing: one teacher used the context of a dolphin. Around a large picture of a dolphin she wrote all the facts the class knew in one colour. As further facts were learnt, they were written alongside in a different colour (*e.g. 'a dolphin sleeps'* became *'a dolphin sleeps with half its brain awake looking for danger'*). Children were engaged and interested in their learning development.

▸ One teacher planned a science week: children first brainstormed what they already knew about caring for the environment, then discussed with talk partners what they wanted to find out – this formed the content of the science week. Children were very enthusiastic and made it clear they wanted to take the lead in the planning. Parents commented on the interest expressed at home.

▸ One teacher asked children to come up with questions to investigate snails and found their questions went far beyond her expectations (e.g. *Where will we find snails? Will they come out at night? Are there water snails in our pond? How do they eat? Where are their mouths? Why do they have a shell?*). Children were highly motivated and engaged, bringing in snails and researching at home and in school.

▸ Prior knowledge about 'Forces' revealed some interesting misconceptions from one teacher (e.g. some children included '*dark forces*' as a result of science fiction influence!)

▸ Learning walls are very common, where children can see what has been covered and what is coming up.

Impact – *as above, plus:*

■ More research at home, using the internet, etc.

■ Teachers don't have to plan so much themselves.

■ Children are making more links in their learning, as the learning is *relevant*.

■ Children are able to tick off and monitor their learning progress.

■ This approach has given children who may be reluctant to contribute the confidence to say when they have found something out, as they feel they are making a valuable contribution.

Years 3 and 4 (8 and 9 year olds)

▸ One teacher said that for five years she had followed the National Curriculum, but had missed out what the pupils are thinking and want to know. She now involves the pupils in planning and adds a final lesson at the end of a unit where pupils can ask questions about what has been learnt.

▸ A teacher at a primary school in East Lothian involves her P4 class (7–8 year olds) in planning by showing them pictures and video to stimulate their thinking. She has found that pupils' ideas match almost exactly the prescribed plans set out by East Lothian Authority. She displays plans – theirs and the prescribed plans – and the pupils use them to see what will be covered next.

'The biggest change since involving them in planning is that they have stopped looking to me for all the answers. They now know that they are capable of finding answers. I have also found that motivation is high from the beginning of the topic to the end. The children are not covering things that they already know, so I am able to extend their learning and let them think "outside the box" for a change. I have also found that my motivation has improved. Every year I will be teaching the topic in a different way: the way that it suits that particular group of children.'

▸ Another teacher used this approach to teach a unit on electricity with her Year 3 class, and had more Level 3s than ever before as a result:

   'Their ideas were permanently displayed on a flipchart. They kept asking what they were going to be learning next. I believe the increased attainment was because they are revising all the time – the flipchart is referred to constantly, so what we learn in each lesson is retained.'

▸ Many teachers reported that they were organising pre-planning discussions with their new classes in the summer term, in readiness for the autumn term, and this had improved the quality of their planning: *'We now start from where the children really are, not from where we think they are.'*

▸ One class, when asked *'What is the key skill you need to learn over time (context: travelling)?'*, told the teacher how they wanted to progress in gymnastics. The pupils came up with what they needed and in what sequence (three ways of travelling at different speeds in a sequence). Their ideas organised the teaching and sequence of lessons.

▸ Post-it notes are often used for extra questions pupils want to ask as the unit is progressing. One pupil wrote, during a unit of work on Judaism, *'Where do Jewish people live?'*, another *'Is marble made of something different to a glass marble?'* during a unit on materials. These misconceptions were noticed and addressed as a result of teachers enabling greater pupil involvement. An example of this approach is shown in Fig. 6.7 for a River Severn topic.

▸ Teachers often said that pupils want to go further than you would have imagined. For example, for a unit including apostrophes, some children asked *'Why is it called an apostrophe? What is the purpose of them? What is its history?'*

▸ One teacher described the problem of giving *too much* freedom in asking pupils how they were going to design a chair for a design technology theme. It became unmanageable because of the wide variety of materials and designs which resulted. He said that next time he would give pupils a selection of possibilities and let them choose within those limits.

Fig. 6.7 River topic questions

▸ Teachers from one team felt that it was vital that weekly plans were not set in stone. The work done by one class as the result of contributing to a local arts celebration had had a very positive impact on one pupil who rarely contributes but knew a lot about Aztecs, the theme of the festival. His input into the planning made his peers re-evaluate him more positively, stimulated them to research more and had a lasting effect on his self-esteem.

Impact – *as above, plus:*

■ Pupils are developing more enquiring minds and better learning skills. More research methods have emerged.

■ Lessons have a faster pace, as units of work are shorter and previously taught sections could be removed.

■ Pupils like to see their progress on the display/poster.

■ Increased motivation anecdote: *'Knowing what happens has had a big impact on achievement and motivation. One boy in my class for the first time brought in good homework not just on time but early.'* (Glasgow Learning Team)

- Because of the greater level of engagement and empowerment, it is now rare to have behaviour problems.

Years 5 and 6 (10 and 11 year olds)

- ▸ One team felt that sometimes cultural change is needed to follow this approach: for instance, one teacher's colleague plans two years in advance, without any consultation with pupils.

- ▸ **A glimpse of how it could be:** one teacher puts next week's planning on the school website on Friday and pupils interact with this before the following week. One pupil emailed the teacher a PowerPoint presentation he had created because he was so enthused about what was to come!

- ▸ One teacher demonstrated how pupils' involvement in planning inspired their confidence and active participation: pupils who had not finished planning how to make a musical instrument asked if they could take their work home, as they wanted to be ready for next week's activities which they had planned and were excited about.

- ▸ Many teachers felt that it was better to display pupils' ideas/coverage as questions, as this leads to a more investigative approach, with an emphasis on processes rather than knowledge.

- ▸ Instead of starting lessons or the day by saying *'What are we doing today?'*, one teacher now avoids this and talks about where they are in their learning journey.

- ▸ Another example of how much further pupils will take things if they are given a chance: given initial minimal coverage about worms, pupils then came up with more penetrating questions than the teacher (e.g. the teacher would have asked *'How do worms move?'* whereas the pupils asked *'Do all worms have the same number of segments?'*)

Impact – *as above, plus:*

- The quality of pupils' questions has improved, because the content has been taken to a deeper level and requires more research.

- More enthusiasm and motivation than before: one pupil's question came up as the focus for a lesson and he exclaimed *'This is my lesson! This is what I want to learn!'*

- Boys' involvement has increased: one teacher allowed pupils to come in before school to work, and at first it was all girls and a few boys, but the more involved the pupils have become in planning, the more boys have opted to participate. This teacher believed that the boys like the research and factual aspects of their learning and were responding to the new level of ownership.

Secondary (12–18)/Special (4–18)

English

▸ One teacher described how student involvement in planning had led to teachers and students having shared language about learning. Teachers are also learning from students as they give blunt but informative feedback when asked what they think of the teacher's planning.

▸ One teacher asked the students at the revision stage for Key Stage 3 national tests (statutory tests for 14 year olds in England) to plan in pairs what they needed. They were asked *'What skills do you want to have by the end of KS3? What will you need to do to get there?'* The students devised a series of lessons together. Teachers said that student involvement in skill progression in this way will help transition from Year 6 (primary) to Year 7 (secondary) as they will not encounter repetition of work.

Art

▸ A Year 12 (17 year olds) art project on the human condition: students were asked to predict what they thought the A-level assessment objectives would look like. Their responses were very close to the real thing. They produced flow diagrams to show the objectives they had come up with, linking the different stages. Students were highly motivated and enthusiastic as a result of their initial involvement.

▸ Having so many classes in a day can cause problems with visual reminders/displays of learning. One strategy is to use pages of a flipchart pad moved from room to room. Moving rooms is the main problem, whereas if a teacher stays in one room then the displays can, of course, be permanent.

Special education

▸ Students in special schools are helped by the continual awareness of how today's lesson fits the big picture. Visual learners are becoming clearer about the purpose of their work.

Impact – *as above, plus:*

■ Increased student ownership.

■ More debate and discussion amongst students.

■ There is greater transference of skills.

Reflection

- Are you satisfied with the level of motivation and enthusiasm in your own class/es or school?
- How far do you believe planning is pitched appropriately in your class/es or school?
- Are there opportunities for pupils to be involved at the pre-planning stage beyond simply stating what they already know and what they want to know, given a broad theme?
- How prescriptive are the contexts for learning (activities and themes) in your class/es or school?
- If you are a senior manager, is there slavish adherence to certain schemes which might be inhibiting pupil progress?
- Which examples or ideas in this chapter have had the greatest impact on your thinking?
- How can you incorporate those new ideas or thoughts into your own planning?
- Do they need further adaptation to fit your particular school, department or class context?

7 What makes effective learning objectives?

6 *It's great because we know what we are doing now and all my learning is expanding!* 9

Nine-year-old

Learning objectives and success criteria are the tools which enable pupils to exercise power over their own learning. Active learners need to be engaged and reflective: success criteria – the ingredients, steps or possible features of the learning objective – provide the rationale for the learning objective in real terms, so that the learner is aware of expectations and can identify which success criteria are going well and which are not.

Once you know exactly where you need help, in whatever form, you are in control of your learning needs. The worst learning scenario is to be unaware of expectations or how your work will be judged and to have no guidelines about how to achieve the objective in the first place.

One of the problems with a set curriculum is that jargon can get in the way of teachers being able to think clearly about what they *really* want pupils to learn in a lesson. Finding half-way through a lesson that pupils are focusing on the wrong thing (e.g. spelling) often occurs when the learning objective itself is wrongly worded. 'To be able to sort shapes', for instance, will lead to a focus on the shapes themselves, whereas 'To use a Venn diagram' will lead to a focus on the sorting process. Both are appropriate, but what matters is the teaching intention.

This chapter and the next deal with the details of learning objectives and success criteria, giving many examples of both – although it is difficult to separate these elements from other formative assessment principles of effective talk and feedback, so inevitably all aspects will overlap.

What we have learnt about learning objectives so far is summarised below:

To plan for effective learning, we know that . . .

- There are often multiple learning objectives in play at any one time (e.g. with **knowledge** a long-term objective, a short-term objective and a related key skill; and with **skills** a long- and a short-term objective).
- **Knowledge** learning objectives need to be explicitly linked with a key skill, so that the success criteria focus on the skill rather than the knowledge.
- **Closed** learning objectives are achieved by simply meeting the success criteria – there are rarely quality issues.
- **Open** learning objectives require discussions with pupils about quality to avoid a minimalistic approach.
- Learning objectives need to be **decontextualised** in order for pupils to be able to transfer them to any context.
- Decontextualised learning objectives promote vocabulary and talk focused on the **learning** rather than the context.

Breaking down learning objectives

Learning objectives tend to be focused either on knowledge *(closed)* or on a skill *(open)*. Many factors are involved in planning, teaching and learning them. When teachers first worked with learning objectives, it was easier to isolate them and deal with them lesson by lesson. However, teachers now see the 'nesting' effect of long- and short-term objectives and how knowledge differs from skills.

Skills usually require no more than a long- and short-term breakdown:

Long term (often several years)	Short term (individual lessons)
To be able to punctuate correctly →	To be able to use question marks
To be able to design a science experiment →	To be able record observations

Knowledge

Knowledge objectives are more complex. We need not only to break them down, but also to link them with a skill, to avoid over-focusing on knowledge and content.

Knowledge learning objectives feature particularly in subjects like history, science and geography, and are also both long term (e.g. to know key events of World War 2) and short term (e.g. to know the properties of a triangle).

There is a danger that if success criteria focus around the short-term knowledge learning objectives (e.g. if success criteria simply list the aspects of the knowledge pupils need to remember), pupils will only have dealt with knowledge. If not in constant use, most knowledge is forgotten. More effective practice is to make explicit the **key skill** which is being used in order to attain that knowledge learning objective, whether it is a key skill within the same subject or not, and to **link the success criteria** with that. Teachers and pupils then focus the lessons on the achievement of the **key skill** as a means of learning facts, thus helping pupils to embed skills that can then be applied in any future context. For many lessons, therefore, there will be an overarching long-term learning objective, a short-term objective and a key skill for this lesson or series of lessons. Some examples of knowledge and linked key-skill learning objectives are given below:

Long-term knowledge objective	Short-term knowledge objective	Key skill (for which success criteria are generated by pupils)
To know all about our local area →	To know where our town is on a map →	To be able to use a map
To know how the human body works →	To know about the senses and their purpose →	To be able to record observations
To know significant events of Tudor times →	To know the impact of Henry VIII's reign on people's lives →	To select and organise historical information
To know the duties of religious leaders →	To know the duties of a Rabbi →	To write a diary

Open and closed learning objectives

Closed learning objectives describe skills which are 'closed' – either right or wrong – such as elements of punctuation, specific algorithms or procedures in mathematics. All *knowledge* learning objectives are closed: you either know the facts or you don't.

Key points about closed learning objectives for formative assessment:

1   *All* the success criteria have to be met for the learning objective to be achieved.

2   There is no difference in *quality* between one pupil's achievement of a closed learning objective and another's (e.g. if we can both use an

index, or say our colours in French, we have attained the learning objective equally and completely). Ticking off that the learning objective has been achieved is at least true for that moment – although whether it will still be achieved in a week's time is another matter, so that form of record keeping is rather unreliable.

3   Feedback, from teacher or pupil, is unlikely to be useful for closed skills if it focuses on the 'success and improvement' strategy (e.g. *Where is my best question mark? How can I improve my question marks?*)! The most effective feedback for closed skills tends to be either a reminder for pupils to check for errors, or more input or teaching of the matter in hand, very often firstly from a talk partner.

Looking for 'success and improvement' does not work, because some pupils may have nothing to improve; for those who do, improvement with closed skills is checking or finding out how to do it; finding the best bits is meaningless when checking the inclusion of success criteria – you either got it or didn't.

Examples of closed learning objectives:

To be able to:	To know:
• use question marks	• the definition of photosynthesis
• catch a ball	• colours in French
• use an index	• key events of the Gunpowder Plot
• subtract using decomposition	• the properties of a square
• read a map	• major rivers in Africa
• use references in an essay	• Pythagoras' theorem

Open learning objectives describe skills for which – even if the success criteria or ingredients have been included – there will always be a difference in quality from one pupil to the next. Two pupils may have included all the elements of a story opening, for instance, yet the quality is different for each. This is when simply ticking off that the learning objective has been attained is meaningless. The learning objectives have been covered and the pupil has begun the process of mastery, but what really matters is how well the pupil has done and what can be improved. Even the most accomplished writer, for example, can always find something to improve; such is the nature of open skills. We want pupils to feel satisfaction with their work when they have analysed it for success and made improvements as best they can, not after their first stab at it. Constant, continual, automatic review and evaluation in order to achieve as well as you can, is the aim of formative assessment.

Key points about open learning objectives for formative assessment:

1   Success criteria may or may not be compulsory ingredients, or they may be elements that simply might help the learner achieve the learning objective (e.g. the different strategies or resources for finding good adjectives, good adverbs, etc).

2   To avoid a minimalistic *'done it!'* approach to success criteria, resulting in minimal quality, there needs to be an opportunity for quality discussion before pupils start to work. Getting the pupils to analyse, via talk partners, two pieces of anonymous finished work of contrasting quality is the most effective technique established so far by learning team teachers. Chapter 9 deals with quality discussions in detail, but the main effect is that the process of comparing one with another (*'Why is this sentence/phrase/effect/ throw, etc, better than this one?'*) powerfully enables pupils to define quality for themselves.

Analysing one finished piece enables pupils to identify the success criteria, but comparing two enables them to define quality in real terms. Excellence for open tasks can take many forms, so to avoid a formulaic approach from only having seen one example of excellence, it is essential that further excellent, *different* examples are also then shown to pupils.

Examples of open learning objectives:

To be able to . . .
- Write a persuasive argument, letter, etc.
- Think of an effective simile, metaphor, personification, etc.
- Solve a numerical/geometric problem.
- Conduct a fair test.
- Compare data, reports, pieces of artwork, different religions, etc.
- Empathise in writing/role play.
- Devise an effective sequence using balance and travelling in gymnastics.
- Use effective adjectives, adverbs, complex sentences, etc.
- Write a characterisation.
- Draw an effective conclusion.

The impact of separating learning objectives from the context of the learning

Making sure that learning objectives do not include the context or activity can, on its own, have a dramatic impact on teaching and learning. To clarify, first, what is meant by a decontextualised learning objective:

The **learning objective** is what you want the pupils to learn:

To write a newspaper report
To analyse data
To be able to multiply by using repeated addition
To be able to paint in the style of Monet

The **context** is simply the activity or vehicle through which the learning objective will be taught:

To write a newspaper report	about pollution in our town (research-based, plus ICT skills)
To analyse data	in comparing climate between Birmingham and Cairo, using atlas graphs
To be able to multiply by using repeated addition	using calculators, Multilink and a variety of resources
To be able to paint in the style of Monet	the scene in our park, first analysing his work and practising the techniques

Problems arise when *both* are combined as one learning objective.

Muddled learning objectives

To write a newspaper report about pollution
To analyse data about climate difference between Birmingham and Cairo
To be able to multiply using repeated addition on a calculator
To be able to paint our park in the style of Monet

If pupils are given a contextualised learning objective, in this way, they over-focus on the most concrete element (e.g. pollution) and their thinking and talk is more likely to be about what they are *doing* rather than what they are *learning*. Secondly, they may believe this skill is only relevant in this context, so don't embed a key skill which can then be transferred to *any* context.

If teachers work with contextualised learning objectives they tend also to over-focus the activity in their planning. Asking pupils to generate success criteria for a pure key skill is plain sailing compared to asking pupils to generate them for a muddled learning objective.

Over several years, teachers in the learning teams have made this their first focus, working in pairs to look at their short-term planning to make sure the learning objectives are separated from the context. The results have been highly significant.

If you make clear which is the learning objective and which is the context, pupils are **able to transfer skills within and across subjects**. Instead of having to start again just because you've changed the context, pupils remember the last time the skill was used and can transfer it to a new and different context (*'We did instructional writing about putting up a tent – we can use it here for what we need for the party'*). They also **use language about the learning objective rather than the context**. This increases pace, means less revisiting and leads to pupils pointing out where skills can be transferred, empowering them as lifelong learners.

As teachers initially can become muddled about which is the learning objective and which is the context, lots of examples and anecdotes about impact across the age groups now follow.

Examples and impact of separating learning objectives from the context of the learning

Nursery/Reception (3, 4 and 5 year olds)

> ▸ Retelling: whereas before children would simply retell the story of *The Three Little Pigs*, now they use story language, like *'once upon a time'* and *'happily ever after'*.

▸ 'Making Father's Day cards' was changed to 'Learning to cut accurately': the result was more attention to the skill and subsequent transferring of that skill.

▸ 'Making treasure maps' was changed to 'Map-making': the quality of work was higher and their talk was about map-making rather than treasure.

▸ 'Making snowflakes' was changed to 'Learning to cut with scissors'. Teaching Assistants behaved differently with the children, saying *'Think how you are using the scissors'* rather than *'What a lovely snowflake you've made.'*

▸ 'Sorting shapes' was changed to 'Using a Venn diagram'. Children talked about the Venn diagrams rather than the shapes.

▸ 'Making robots' became 'Using joining skills', so junk modelling focused around joining rather than talk about robots.

Years I and 2 (6 and 7 year olds)

▸ One teacher focused on 'explanation' – being able to explain – with the context of a car travelling down a ramp: the children were able to explain very clearly what they had learnt. A parallel teacher had taught the same lesson, but had made the learning objective 'making a car go down a ramp': those pupils could only say things like *'I made a car whiz down the ramp!'*

▸ One class focused on information writing, with the context of dinosaurs. A few weeks later, the pupils remembered the success criteria and were able to transfer the skill to a different context, of elephants.

Years 3 and 4 (8 and 9 year olds)

▸ One class covered explanatory texts in literacy, and were able to transfer this skill to a science report on how rocks are formed.

▸ One teacher changed 'Taking the temperature between our toes' to 'Reading a thermometer' with the context of 'hot parts of the body'.

▸ A teacher started a unit on persuasive language with the context of making a poster. She asked the class for ideas for the context which resulted in her scrapping her planning and focusing the whole unit around the context of the TV programme *The Apprentice*. They were highly motivated yet focused on the skills involved.

▸ In a PE lesson, a teacher emphasised the sequencing involved in floor work, which the children were then able to transfer to large apparatus. (Usually she had to start again, because it all looks so different.)

Years 5 and 6 (10 and 11 year olds)

▸ A pupil with Asperger's Syndrome told the teacher that the learning objective had made him happy, because he could think about what he was going to learn.

▸ One teacher did the same lesson twice, once with the learning objective decontextualised and once with the context included:

Context included: they were asked to write the story of Goldilocks from a different perspective. The pupils got sidetracked with the features of the tale, like details about the characters, and did not adequately include a different perspective.

Decontextualised: for another lesson, she asked the pupils to generate success criteria, from a given piece of work, for 'Writing a traditional tale from a different perspective'. It was as if a light had been switched on. There was a dramatic impact on the quality of their writing. The teacher later tried the same thing in history and found the same thing happened.

▸ One child in a special school was asked what she thought about having learning objectives. She said *'It's great because when you go to the loo, you remember what you were doing when you come back.'*

▸ Pupils wrote a non-chronological report about St Lucia. When they later had to write a report about the countries taking part in the World Cup, they were immediately able to use all the skills learnt from the previous report.

▸ Writing a persuasive leaflet for a Key Stage 2 national test, one pupil recognised that he had done something like this before and said *'This is exactly the same but a different subject!'*

▸ Teachers in one team felt that they had moved away from 'doing the Romans' and were now looking at a set of skills within that context.

▸ One teacher had a key skills geography curriculum and was using the context of rainforests. When this had been covered without key skills in the past, the pupils would end up knowing a lot about trees and animals, but have no understanding of the geography skills involved. They studied a local area for a week and then showed pupils images of the rainforest. Pupils were able then to identify the positive and negative aspects of the rainforest and were using geographical vocabulary instead of context vocabulary.

▸ In history, 'Designing an Egyptian banquet menu' was changed to 'To know what foods the Egyptians ate', with the context of designing a banquet menu. In the past they had focused on the creation of the menu, but with the new learning objective they understood what they were learning.

▸ Instead of focusing RE objectives on individual religions and having to start again each time, one teacher used the objective 'Why people worship' with the context of different religions. Pupils were able to see the links between lessons, even though the context changed.

▸ After doing estimation and measuring with angles, a class then did the same with capacity. Because the focus was estimating and measuring, they were not scared by a new context, and gained confidence as a result.

Secondary (12–18 year olds)

Physics

▸ One teacher found that students could now recognise the same skill being practised again in a different context (e.g. transport, electricity, etc).

Mathematics

▸ One teacher from the North Yorkshire Learning Team changed 'Finding the area of shapes' to 'Applying a formula to find the area of shapes'. Each lesson dealt with a different shape but a formula was being applied each time, which was a more successful approach. This had made students more independent.

'In Year 10 you deal with the same formula in different contexts all the time. Before I separated the learning objective from the context, students did not realise they could use the same formula across different aspects of mathematics. I think you could cut down the number of maths teaching objectives considerably by focusing on transferring the same formula.'

English

▸ An objective of 'expressing empathy' meant that students were clear about what they had to do and did not get bogged down with the wrong things.

▸ In a special school, a Year 9 class was reading Macbeth for the Key Stage 3 national test. The students focused on the research and presentation skills involved. Weeks later, a science teacher, working with a completely different context, said that the students' research and presentation skills were excellent and they had told her about how they had done this in their English class.

▸ In one school, 80 per cent of Key Stage 4 students increased their grades by at least one as a result of this strategy and the use of success criteria.

▸ Greater student independence and confidence brought a positive impact on behaviour.

Reflection

- How far do pupils talk about skills they are learning rather than knowledge they have gained?
- Do your learning objectives include the context?
- Are some easier to separate than others?
- What do your pupils say when you ask them what they are learning?
- Are there systems in place in your class/school which tell a pupil when a learning objective is achieved?
- How valid, reliable or useful are such systems?
- Is there a clear understanding of the difference between open and closed skills in your class/school?
- When teaching knowledge, can you identify the key skill being used during the lesson?
- Do you ever find yourself starting again with skills already taught because the context is different?
- How far can your pupils transfer skills from context to context?

8 How will we know what learning objectives mean?

> 6 I think success criteria help me because I know what I need to do, and what I need to do to improve my own work. 9
>
> *Eight-year-old*

Although success criteria have been referred to constantly so far, we now need to look closely at the issues surrounding their generation and use. Success criteria are the ingredients of the learning objective. For **closed learning objectives**, they are often chronological and are always compulsory (e.g. the steps in a mathematics algorithm or the ingredients needed for instructional writing). For **open learning objectives**, they can be compulsory elements, such as the aspects needed in a fair test, or they might be things that you *could* include (e.g. the possible elements in a good characterisation). Using success criteria has had a major impact on both teaching and learning, but mainly in equipping pupils with the tools to be able to self- and peer-assess.

What we have learnt about success criteria so far:

In order to have maximum impact, success criteria . . .

- Need to be known, in a basic form, by teachers first.
- Should be the same for all learners in a class – differentiation by access should be sought via the amount of support provided within the activity.
- Must be generated by pupils, or they have little meaning and less impact on learning.
- Can be used across the curriculum, including social skills, thinking skills, etc.
- Need to be constantly referred to by pupils and ticked off for closed skills.
- For open skills, need to be checked for inclusion first, but then used to decide on most successful and where to improve (see Chapter 9).
- One success criterion can be used as the focus for a lesson, broken down into further success criteria.
- Need to be part of a bigger picture in defining quality: open, creative work might be more or less than the 'sum of its parts' (Sadler, 1989).

Differentiation

Some authorities advocate '*must, should, could*' as the basis for three lists of differentiated success criteria, to ensure that all pupils progress. All the teachers in learning teams using this method have found it constrained pupils, lowered their expectations and overloaded short-term planning, so have now abandoned this approach. Differentiation by activity, rather than differentiating by success criteria, seems more successful.

It is most effective if all pupils have the same learning objective, the same context and the same success criteria, but certain success criteria are highlighted as priorities and, most importantly, activities are planned so that there is varied support within the task to ensure authentic 'personalised learning'. For instance, where some pupils might be free-writing against success criteria, others might be working on a partially completed text. Varying the response required in the activity would be another example (e.g. written/spoken, as a podcast, etc). Challenging higher achievers seems to be best achieved through the original analysis of excellent work of a higher level (see Chapter 9). With open skills, everyone can go further, but they need to know what that might look like.

Pupil generation of success criteria

We have learnt that success criteria must be generated by pupils to have maximum impact. There are now several very high-quality techniques for not only getting pupils to generate success criteria, but also for helping them understand what excellence looks like for the learning objective in focus.

Effective techniques

1 Especially effective for young children: ask '*Can you. . . (e.g. count these cubes)?*' To the answer '*Yes!*', ask the children to **prove it**, by saying what they would need to do first, then next and so on. A more structured strategy is to demonstrate something being done (making sure you **do it wrong**) and let the children call out to tell you what you are doing wrong and what should be done instead. (Both strategies first described by members of the Essex Learning Team.)

2 **A finished piece of work** for this lesson from a previous/parallel class is projected or photocopied and given out at the beginning of the lesson. Although the teacher can 'create' this, there is more impact if the work

is clearly from another pupil. Children are fascinated and engaged by previous pupil work and are inspired: they believe that it is then possible for them to do the same or even better. The work is analysed, via talk partners, for what can be seen: e.g. *'One minute to decide one thing you can see in this work to do with persuasion.'* It is important to state the learning objective, or pupils simply tell you about spelling and neatness.

This technique works well with anything written, with large pieces of artwork or DT models or photographs which can be projected via the laptop. The success criteria are generated and pupils have a clear idea of expectations and the 'big picture'. Copying is not an issue – two years of trialling across the learning teams show the reverse to be true: children do not copy except in the case of the very lowest achievers, whose work is then better than it would have been. Instead, pupils are inspired by what they see.

By far the best device for projecting work or anything instantly is a *Visualiser*. This is a video camera on a tabletop stand. Anything laid underneath the camera is projected on a screen instantly, whether it is a 3D object or a piece of writing. Chapter 9 gives more detail about the impact of using a visualiser in modelling the success and improvement approach within lessons.

3   **Two pieces of finished work**, of differing quality, are projected side by side or given out. The paired analysis focuses first of all on the features seen (the success criteria) and then on which of the two pieces best fulfils each of the success criteria. For open skills, this technique gives pupils the chance not only to generate success criteria, but also to develop a deep understanding of what quality would mean for those success criteria. Chapter 7 deals with quality issues in depth.

   Word of warning: for creative subjects, it is important to avoid confining pupils to the models shown – so there should be a number of different examples available for pupils to see, for instance, how there is no single way of writing a good story opening or evoking a mood in paint. The detailed analysis of two pieces or products deepens their understanding, which can be deepened still further if they encounter a variety of different approaches which still meet the success criteria.

4   For mathematics: on the board show the learning objective, **poor-quality success criteria**, and two calculations both completed wrongly. Get the pupils to discuss in talk partners what has gone wrong, making the important point that the success criteria have all been met yet the maths has gone wrong. Pupils can then determine the correct, necessary success criteria to use for their work.

5   For some key skills, a finished product shown at the beginning is not the best vehicle for generating the success criteria, because the processes involved are not visible in the finished product. The most effective approaches so far are (*a*) to **demonstrate** while pupils, in pairs, write possible success criteria; and (*b*) to give the class a task (*e.g. comparing three different graphs for the key skill of analysing and comparing data*) then stop at frequent intervals, asking them to describe exactly what they have had to do so far (*'What did you do first? Exactly what did you do? Then next?. . .'.*). This is a **retrospective creation of success criteria**. Once the list of processes has been made, it can then be used over and over again and modified as necessary.

6   **Revisit existing success criteria** after the task in hand is completed and ask pupils if they want to modify them in any way in the light of their experience of working with them. This might mean removing, adding more, amending or giving examples to make the criteria easier.

Once success criteria have been generated by pupils, they can be made into A5 cards, A4 sheets in folders, posters on walls, stored on interactive whiteboards/in Smart notebooks, etc, and used whenever that skill recurs. Pure, decontextualised learning objectives lead to generic success criteria, which can be used in any context, so this should be the aim when generating them – otherwise their shelf life is too short and pupils do not see the vital link between and within subjects when skills are transferred.

Breaking success criteria down for closer focus

Broad key skills produce broad success criteria, so it can often be necessary to take each of the success criteria in turn and make those the focus of a lesson or series of lessons. 'Persuasive writing' would be a good example of this, where each element is worthy of a number of lessons:

To write a persuasive argument	Letter to local MP	• A statement of your viewpoint • A number of reasons for this, with evidence • A number of reasons from an alternative standpoint • Attempts at striking up empathy with the recipient • Recommended alternative action • A summary • Reasoning connectives

We could take 'striking up empathy' for instance, present pupils with two contrasting examples of persuasive letters – one which empathises well and one which doesn't – and get them to analyse the pieces in order to generate success criteria for empathy: we might find *'flattery'*, *'mentioning something the recipient is personally connected with'*, *'appealing to his/her better nature'* and so on.

One possible lesson pathway

It is impossible and undesirable to set out a rigid path for the format of every lesson, but there are some clear links and pathways once success criteria become part of everyday teaching.

The following pathway demonstrates a common journey through a lesson or series of lessons, for which learning objectives and the generating of success criteria is usually the first step. Success criteria are then used throughout the lesson for different purposes.

Before the lesson
- Learning objectives for lesson planned in the short term.
- Success criteria thought about by teacher.
- Good and not so good anonymous examples of finished products are found (e.g. written work, artwork, 3D objects, photographs of things too bulky to store, video clips of PE or games skills, video clips of drama, etc).

During the lesson
- Teacher refers to whole unit coverage, stating what learning has taken place so far and where it is now.
- A good formative question is asked which will get the pupils thinking and discussing the subject matter of the learning objective in talk partners, their responses revealing their understanding and misconceptions (see Chapter 5 for ideas about effective questioning).
- The two examples of contrasting previous work are projected/shared with the class visually for initial class analysis with talk partners to:
  (a) determine success criteria *(What can you see?)*; and, for open skills only,
  (b) identify quality through comparing the two pieces against those success criteria *(Why is this sentence/aspect better than this one?)*.
- Pupils' work takes place, with continual checking against the success criteria.
- Once, twice or more, a random pupil's work is projected at the front, there and then, and pupils, in pairs, analyse it for success and improvement needs, suggesting actual improvements which are then made as a class.
- Using this as a model, the pupils then identify success and make improvements in their own work, working on their own or via paired discussions.
- Lesson ends with summary of learning, examples of improvements made and reference to the next learning focus.

This pathway demonstrates the central role of the success criteria in helping pupils know what to do, giving them ownership of the ingredients of the skill in focus, and giving them the basis of self- and peer-evaluation. An understanding of quality is most effective when it originates from analysis of work – whether from a previous or different class or from someone's work chosen randomly while the lesson is in progress – and the analysis made against the success criteria.

Success criteria are the foundation for pupils being enabled to become active learners, so I have provided a wealth of examples of use and impact throughout this book, in order to further and deepen teachers' understanding. These examples demonstrate not only high-quality teaching and learning, but also many innovative ideas and techniques for engaging pupils actively in generating and using success criteria for maximum effect. More examples will be found in Chapters 9 and 10, as success criteria are central also to quality issues and self- and peer-feedback.

Examples of success criteria techniques: their use and impact

Nursery/Reception (3, 4 and 5 year olds)

Techniques and use

▸ Success criteria for nursery classes are often more usefully adopted by all the adults involved, rather than children, in order to inform the quality of their talk with children. If the adults have a clear understanding of all the learning objectives for the different skills involved (e.g. building, nesting, etc, as well as social skills), then whatever a child does, the adult will have the knowledge of the success criteria to be able to ask appropriate questions. This means teachers can still follow children's interests, but the talk will be appropriate.

▸ Teachers of this age group find transferable social skills – such as turn-taking, good listening, etc – work very well as success criteria.

▸ One teacher used success criteria for 'going to the toilet' after her 4-year-old boys continually left the toilets in a terrible mess. Children now see a mess and report it, telling the teacher how the mess was made, according to the very explicit success criteria! This has resulted in wonderfully clean toilets.

> ▸ It is easier to get children of this age to generate success criteria for closed skills. Given a story opening, for instance, it is difficult for them to pick out features. They simply want to comment on the story.

> ▸ Using a puppet to share success criteria proved very successful at Nursery/Reception and led to children telling each other what they were supposed to be doing.

> ▸ The key at this age is to be as visual (and as humorous) as possible. One teacher drew a self-portrait on the board with missing features: the children in pairs had to discuss what was missing, and from this they drew up the success criteria. Children worked against the success criteria and were overheard telling each other what to include.

> ▸ At this stage there are so many things you want them to remember about writing, it is important to separate the technical skills from specific learning objectives. Using a poster of long-term skills like 'finger spaces' and so on is very useful.

> ▸ Fig. 8.1 shows examples of success criteria generated by children and written on A3 templates, photocopied and used in subsequent lessons by the children to guide their learning and enable them to self- and peer-evaluate.

Impact

- Using success criteria raises self-esteem because children know when they have achieved success and get positive and immediate self-gratification.

- Children are more secure and confident; quality of work is better, teaching and learning is at a quicker pace, children can use the success criteria for self- and peer-evaluation.

- In one reception class, the teacher had previously asked for 'thumbs up' for success. With the advent of success criteria, one child said 'We need words', indicating that she needed to describe her achievements more thoroughly than with a yes/no approach.

- Children are not as scared of making mistakes, as a result of seeing varying work at the beginning of the lesson when they generate the success criteria.

- Children are really proud of their work: they verbalise their success and don't need to be told they have done it right or 'well done' because they self-mark. In one class, children told the teacher this was the best work they had ever done, referring to their achievement.

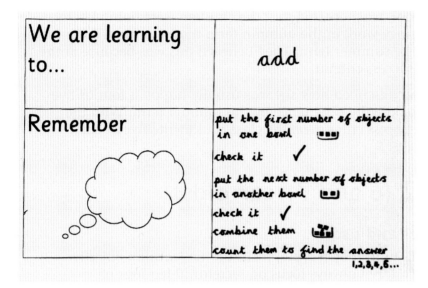

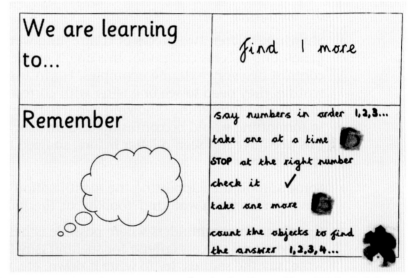

Fig. 8.1 A3 success criteria templates (with thanks to Bec Wakefield)

- There is less time-wasting and children get going with their work without asking questions.

- Teachers are more freed up, so there is more time to listen to children and intervene.

- In one Scottish school, eight children in Primary 1 passed the national writing tests. These teachers had never had such a high number and believed success criteria were the key to their success (generating them, seeing previous work, doing self- and peer-feedback using the criteria, etc).

- In one school, teachers said that the children were doing Literacy and Numeracy work in the autumn term that was usually done in the following summer term. They believed this was because of the impact of success criteria.

- One teacher described how she was usually happy if four or five children could write a sentence by the summer term. With the advent of success criteria, *all* the class could write five or six sentences.

Years 1 and 2 (6 and 7 year olds)

Techniques and use

▸ To begin with, until they learn to focus on the learning objective in question, children always focus on secretarial features of writing when asked to generate success criteria, so this has to be discouraged.

▸ Showing children two pieces of contrasting work as a means of their generating success criteria for this age is very effective, but needs to contrast two very extreme examples. For instance, if focusing on letter writing, they need to see one letter with correct formatting and one that has no formatting. Showing two letters with only some differences in formatting would be confusing and unclear, as many children of this age have not seen a letter before, so need the 'right and wrong' starting point.

▸ Some schools are supporting the identification of success criteria by having a learning wall and 'toolkits' as the success criteria.

▸ Creating visual reminders where possible is helpful. One teacher created visual success criteria for spelling (say the word you want to write, say the sounds, try to write it down, etc, with illustrative drawings).

▸ The following description is the summary of an English lesson for Years 1 and 2, taught by Julie Jones, in Powys:

Learning objective: To learn how to make a clear poster

Julie first began the lesson by 'randomly' selecting three of the posters last year's class had made for the Christmas Fair. They took each in turn and discussed what was good about the poster and what could be improved. Lucy's work was first (see Fig. 8.2): the class decided it was bright and had nice Christmas trees, but the letters were 'a bit funny' in places. Natalie's work was next (see Fig.8.3): they liked the reindeer drawing on the right and the neat writing, but suggested that the yellow drawings could be missed out because they didn't stand out. Julie pointed out that, without the date, there could be trouble!

Fig. 8.2 Lucy's poster

Fig. 8.3 Natalie's poster

They then looked at Jeena's poster (see Fig. 8.4) and were asked to say which was the easier of the three to read. They agreed it was Jeena's and then worked with their talk partner to list what made her poster clear. They were not to discuss how the posters could be improved, just what made this one easiest to read. Their comments formed the success criteria:

Fig. 8.4 Jeena's poster

Success criteria
- Make all your letters the same size.
- Use dark colours.
- Don't use yellow.
- Put pictures round the edge, not in the middle.
- Check that you have copied all the words and numbers.

Julie then asked the class to make posters for the Christmas concert, put the facts about the concert on the board for them to copy (so the focus was not on spelling), and reminded them to use capitals for all the words and to pencil in the letters first.

As they worked, Julie kept reminding them of the success criteria. *'When I looked at the finished posters I was delighted with the end results. The posters were all easier to read – the writing was simply coloured and much more effective'* (see Zoe's poster – Fig. 8.5).

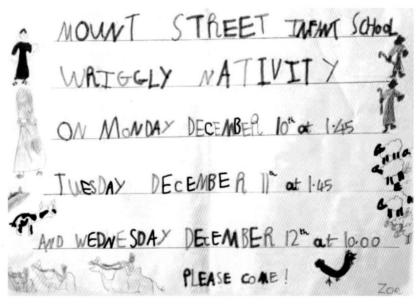

Fig. 8.5 Zoe's poster

▸ Fig. 8.6 is a self-assessment grid created for handwriting skills using success criteria generated by children. Children refer to these criteria and 'traffic light' new grids regularly to keep track of their handwriting progress, and find them very focusing.

Impact – *as above, plus:*

■ Success criteria have a significant impact on children's writing, compared to other subjects where success criteria have been used.

Using Success Criteria in Hand Writing

Pupil	Success Criteria	Miss
●	Joined letters	
	Letters sitting on line	
●	Tall letters straight	
	Correct spacing	
	Letters formed correctly	
●	All small letters same size	
●	Use a sharp pencil	
●	Don't press down too hard	
	Not too big/too small	
●	Dot the i	
	Straight tails	
●	Tails below the line	
●	Use rubber for mistakes	
	Do not rush your work	

Pupil	Success Criteria	Miss
●	Joined letters	
	Letters sitting on line	
●	Tall letters straight	
●	Correct spacing	
●	Letters formed correctly	
	All small letters same size	
●	Use a sharp pencil	
●	Don't press down too hard	
	Not too big/too small	
●	Dot the i	
	Straight tails	
●	Tails below the line	
●	Use rubber for mistakes	
●	Do not rush your work	

Fig. 8.6 Self-assessment handwriting grid (with thanks to Lisa Richards)

■ Children are inspired by seeing a child's previous work and want to do better.

■ Children are more independent.

■ Checking against success criteria has led to a culture of constant review. Teachers are seeing more insertions, crossings-out and self-corrections in children's work. *'Just looking at these very young people checking to see what they have or have not done is unbelievable.'*

Years 3 and 4 (8 and 9 year olds)

Techniques and use

▸ Teachers have found it very successful to move on from *'must, should, could'* criteria, as pupils can now aim higher. Teachers also now have higher expectations.

▸ A PE teacher gets the pupils to plan movements and talk about them in talk partners, and videos the pupils making the movements so that they can self-assess. This has been very successful in making the pupils more evaluative.

▸ At this age, success criteria can be 'fine-tuned' after using them, in the light of how useful they were.

> ▸ Teachers and numeracy consultants in Devon wrote the following piece about the importance of incorporating Attainment Target 1 (Using & Applying) in mathematics where appropriate.

Success criteria in mathematics lessons (ALL PHASES)

Including decision making

Reasoning and decision making are fundamental to mathematical thinking and should therefore be inherent in success criteria. Success criteria can easily become a set of algorithmic, procedural instructions. For example, when teaching subtraction, using the number line to find the difference between two numbers, success criteria could look different with/without reasoning:

Algorithmic/no decision making	Incorporating decision making
• Write the smaller number on the left-hand side of the number line. • Write the larger number at the other end. • Jump to the nearest multiple of ten. • Jump up in tens until you get to the multiple of ten just before the larger number. • Jump to the large number. • Remember to label your jumps. • Add up the jumps.	• Decide which numbers and where to put them on your number line. • Count between the numbers as efficiently as you can. • Is your answer what you are expecting? • Check your answers with your partner every so often and make sure you agree on the answers.

This is not to say that you would not model the approach to counting-on outlined above, but, if teaching focuses on understanding of subtraction and how the number line can support subtraction calculations, the children who understand subtraction will not need to follow step-by-step instructions. Therefore, those children who are not able to use the number line almost certainly don't understand, and following step-by-step instructions can mask this lack of understanding.

Thus, the success criteria could all have an element of decision making, checking and communicating about them, and could therefore have generic phrases. Success criteria like these could be displayed on a working wall:

> Do you need to check/have you checked/how will you check?
> Decide if it will help to use jottings or record in any way.
> Decide if it will help to use a resource.
> Think if there is more than one way to approach the problem. . . which would be most efficient?
> Look at the numbers. . .
> Have you thought about what you know that might help. . . ?
> etc

▶ The following description is of an English Year 4 lesson taught by Kathryn Atkinson (North Tyneside Learning Team):

Learning objective: To be able to write a clear set of instructions

Context: By making a box guitar (linking to a science topic on sound)

After initial introduction to the learning objective, the children were shown three examples of Year 6 pupils' instructional writing and were given two minutes with talk partners to compile ideas about the features of instructional writing. Ideas were shared and the success criteria (or 'X Factor' in this class!) were generated:

The children were then given a poor set of instructions for making a box guitar and tried to follow them, annotating and making improvements to them as they proceeded.

Success criteria generated by children:
- Title
- What you need
- How to make
- Numbers
- Bullet points
- Verbs
- Time connectives
- Diagrams

After a discussion about following poor instructions and how they could be improved, the children set about writing their own instructions. They were then able to make their own box guitars by following their *talk partner's* instructions. This allowed them all to peer-mark their partner's work according to the success criteria.

'The lesson was extremely successful and the children produced the best set of instructions they had all year.'

▶ Charlotte Smith's class (Lincoln Learning Team) produced these success criteria for writing an autobiography:

Learning objective: To be able to write an autobiography

Context: Myself

Success criteria:

- Use first person
- Include your feelings
- Add complex sentences
- Include an introduction that hooks the reader
- Include adventurous language
- Include at least one simile
- Interest the reader by adding as much detail as possible.

Impact – *as above, plus:*

- Success criteria for writing are now in the children's heads for many frequently-used aspects, so the children do not refer to them, but remember them.

- Success criteria enable children to identify errors at an early stage. One teacher described a less confident child saying *'Wow! I didn't think I could do such a good piece of work and I got it finished!'*

- Overheard from a group of low achievers in a mathematics lesson: *'My answer's different to yours.' 'That's because you've missed out step 2.'* There had been significant progress for all children as a result of being able to isolate exactly where they needed to seek help or improve something.

- End-of-year results had improved in one school. Teachers believed this was a direct result of success criteria and their use.

Years 5 and 6 (10 and 11 year olds)

Techniques and use

▸ One teacher found that he often had success criteria in mind at the start of the week, but after talking to the pupils realised that some of the criteria can be broken down again to make things really clear. This was a way of differentiating and raising expectation at the same time.

▸ Some teachers keep their short-term plans, including pupil-generated success criteria, on the laptop, so that they can be displayed on the interactive whiteboard when needed.

▸ By this age, many pupils have success criteria embedded, and will quickly write them from memory in the margin of their work before they start.

▸ The following examples of success criteria for the key skills of writing a balanced argument, a persuasive piece and diary-writing (Fig. 8.7) were generated by pupils from teachers in the Dorset Learning Team:

Learning objective: To write a balanced argument

Context: Any topic or subject

Success criteria:
- Equal number of points for and against.
- Number the points.
- Prioritise points in order of importance.
- Present tense.
- Statistics.

Learning objective: To write a point of view or persuasive argument

Context: Any topic or subject

Success criteria:
- Reason for your writing.
- Express your view.
- Paragraphs to persuade.
- Connectives.
- Emotive language.
- Conclusion.

Learning objective: To write a diary (see Fig. 8.7)

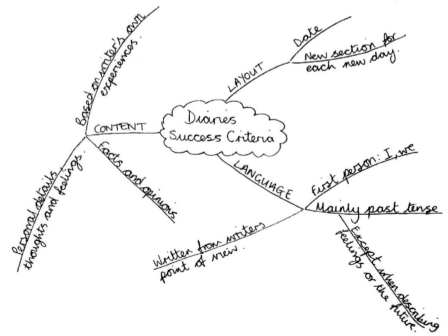

Fig. 8.7 Diary-writing success criteria

▶ The following three Year 6 lesson descriptions are from Emma Bradshaw, in the Essex Learning Team: first an art lesson, then spelling, then mathematics.

ART LESSON

Learning objective: To blend watercolour paints and pencils to create a 3D effect (a closed, specific technique)

Context: Poppies

Fig. 8.8 Teacher's poppy

Emma modelled her own painting (Fig. 8.8) by demonstrating, stage by stage, drawing, painting, then adding detail with watercolour pencils. As the pupils observed, they were asked to think about the techniques the teacher was using. After each stage, success criteria were drawn up and discussed before the pupils completed their own poppies.

Success criteria generated by pupils:

Drawing:	Painting:	Watercolour pencil:
• Use pencil lightly to begin with • Fill the whole piece of paper • Use flowing lines • Overlap the petals	• Use only red, orange, black, white and green • Make sure the brush is not too wet • Complete one petal at a time • Use dark paint on overlapping edges and red paint on outside edges of petals and blend them in the middle • Work quickly and blend colours while they are still wet	• Use only black and brown • Make 'textured' marks • Use only a small amount

The success criteria were written up on the board for the class to refer to. At various stages in the lesson the pupils were asked to complete a 'gallery' activity. All work was left on display and the pupils had to select the 'best' ones for achievement of the success criteria. Discussion of the 'hardest' success criteria also took place, and pupils who had been successful gave their suggestions to others who were having difficulties.

Examples of poppies created by children can be seen in Fig. 8.9.

Fig. 8.9 Two pupils' poppies

SPELLING LESSON

Learning objective: To know and use a variety of spelling strategies

Context: A B C D Word Game

The children drew up a list of success criteria for spelling:

Success criteria:
- Use a rule that you already know.
- Think of other words with the same spelling pattern.
- Look for smaller words within the word.
- Look at the word carefully – does it look right?
- Count the syllables.
- Sound it out.
- Use mnemonics *(big elephants can. . .)* to remember difficult spellings.

With this game, four choices of spelling for a word are given. Talk partners discuss which is the correct spelling and which success criteria they can use to help them to make the right choice.

A architeture   B arcitecture   C architecture ✔   D arckitecture

Pupils decide the correct spelling and share the success criteria they found most useful in helping them to make their decision.

MATHEMATICS LESSON

Learning objective: To solve mathematical word problems

Context: Given word problems

Pupils completed one example of a word problem with their talk partners, then discussed the process they had worked through. They then shared ideas with the rest of the class and came up with a list of agreed success criteria:

Success criteria for answering problems:
- Read the question twice.
- Underline key words.
- Decide which operation to use.
- Estimate the answer.
- Choose method: mental, pencil and paper, or calculator.
- Do calculation and interpret answer.
- Include any units (e.g. kg, cm.).
- Check the answer.

The pupils also came up with a list of tips:

Remember . . . if you are stuck, you could:
- Describe the problem in your own words to a partner.
- Talk through what you have done so far.
- Break the problem into smaller steps.
- Draw something to help you (e.g. number line).
- Make a guess and see if it works! If not try to improve it.

▸ James Crump, from West Sussex, was interested in pupils becoming more aware of exactly what success criteria meant. Even though they had generated them, he felt that they needed examples to refer to in order to aim for the highest quality. Some teachers get examples of quality from two contrasting pieces used for analysis at the beginning of the lesson, but James tried a different approach. By analysing a number of excellent texts about survival stories, together with his Year 6 class, generic 'Wow!' factor success criteria were formed for writing. To exemplify the criteria, they then chose appropriate quotes from the text. The *Wow!* criteria are permanently displayed in the classroom, and can be slotted in to any other list of criteria (see Figure 8.10).

Generic *Wow!* factor success criteria

- **Always use a comma wisely – they are so powerful!**
  And that, I know, always helps.
  I do not feel entirely lost, as I am on the way to better things, situations where I do not feel so alone, when I awake with a smile.
  Muldoon pitched backwards, his spine arched, his arms flung outwards.
  I know about life, I have cheated death, come walk with me, I'll tell you my story.
  Through the fog, not far away now, I could sense them coming.
- **Short sentences for effect:**
  I squirmed on my hard seat. Never again. Never again.
  It bounces. Fine.
  I am lost.
  What a day! Will this ever end?
- **Varied sentence lengths**
- **Questions:**
  You know what thought?
  And I ask myself, why has this happened?
- **Simile:**
  The teacher, like a vulture, descended upon the exams, sank his talons into their pages, ripped the answers to shreds and then, perching in his chair, began to digest.
- **Personification:**
  The classroom froze around me.
  The chairs and tables smiled a satisfying smile.
  The outfit screamed 'I am cool!'
- **Paragraphs**
- **Time connectives:**
  next, later, then, after, before, first, at the same time, as soon as she left, late on Friday, when I finished, consequently, suddenly, finally, out of the blue, meanwhile, earlier on.
- **Verbs (action words):**
  strolling, gazing, sprinting, chuckling, bellowed, panting, collapsed, leapt, glided, skidded, slumped, strode, soared
- **Use adverbs to further describe your verbs:**
  casually strolling, silently crept
- **Use bodily response to describe your feelings or how you react to something:**
  Blood flushed in my cheeks.
  My lips turned blue.
  An icicle hung from my nose.

Empathy success criteria:

- Talk as though you are in the shoes of a different person.
- It must be written in the first person *(What am I doing here?)*.
- Express and emphasise your feelings.
- Make the reader really feel as though you are talking directly to them or that as the reader you are inside the mind of that person.
- Present tense.
- *Wow!* criteria.
- Questioning.
- Reflection – look back and express your thoughts.

Fig. 8.10 Empathy writing by a low achiever using *Wow!* success criteria

Impact *– as above, plus:*

- In one school, attainment levels went up from 87% to 92%. In this school, pupils ask for help and extra work for success criteria which they feel they have not achieved. This is seen as a huge leap in confidence from the previous mindset of *'I'm no good at this'*.

- Test results in one learning team were higher than ever before. Teachers believed that success criteria were a significant factor. Some teachers believe that success criteria have had a greater impact on higher achievers.

- A child on the SEN register said *'Do they do success criteria in secondary schools, because I really know what I'm doing with them?'* In one IEP box he had previously written, in answer to 'What helps you learn?', *'Not annoying people around me'*. This time he had written *'Success criteria help me learn.'*

- The focus of success criteria improves pupil behaviour.

Secondary (12–18 year olds)

Techniques and use

▸ One teacher used old test mark schemes to help students understand success criteria and the difference between levels. This helped their confidence and understanding.

▸ One PE teacher used moderated video examples to ask students why the PE shown was successful and how it met criteria. They were then able, in pairs, to assess their own work against this.

▸ Stella Gillett, from the Powys Learning Team, used success criteria for the first time for two Year 8 RE lessons. The students generated the following criteria, through much talk-partner discussion.

RELIGIOUS EDUCATION

Learning objective: To understand religious attitudes to environmental issues

Context: A newspaper article and an oral presentation

Success criteria for a newspaper article:	Success criteria for an oral presentation:
• A summary (of a topic on danger to the environment)	• A brief history of the topic
• A reference to the subject (local environment)	• How it is affecting the subject (the environment)
• At least two contrasting opinions (information on how at least two religions view environmental issues)	• Possible solutions to the problem
	• References to opinion (religious opinion or teaching)

Pupil comment: *'This is really interesting stuff. Better than just reading and answering the questions.'*

Learning objective: To produce a travel brochure

Context: To a place of pilgrimage

Success criteria:
- The history of the place
- Places of special interest
- Places to stay
- Reasons for visiting (religious and spiritual)
- Correct presentation

Pupil comment: *'It really helped when we talked about what should be in it because I wasn't too sure at first.'*

▸ Aurore Foti, from the North Tyneside Learning Team, describes the following stages in the lead up to a 'café conversation' as a model of her Year 8 students' oral French ability at the end of a unit on 'food and drink', using success criteria for the first time.

MODERN FOREIGN LANGUAGES: FRENCH

Lesson 1: reading comprehension activities on 'café conversations'.

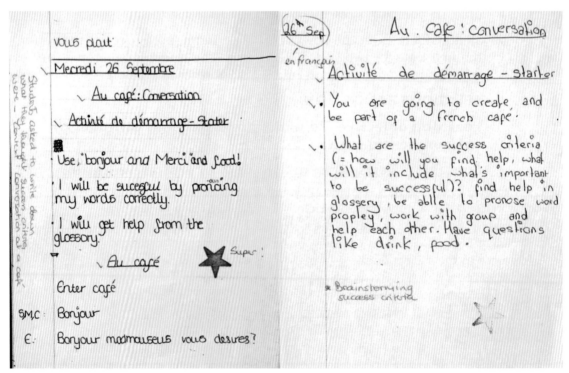

Fig. 8.11 French conversation success criteria

Lesson 2: students were asked to brainstorm good/essential ingredients for a great oral performance. Fig. 8.11 shows two typical examples.

Students then went into groups and planned their café conversation together, using their success criteria. *'Fantastic achievement, impact on motivation, wanting to do well. Some rehearsed it at home too!'*

Lesson 3: the class brainstormed assessment criteria in relation to the success criteria, and produced a grid including marks to help them produce more detailed feedback and targets for improvement. As each group performed, the rest of the class was given two minutes to write up their feedback and then share it with the class. Groups also assessed their own performance. An example of an assessment grid is shown in Fig. 8.12.

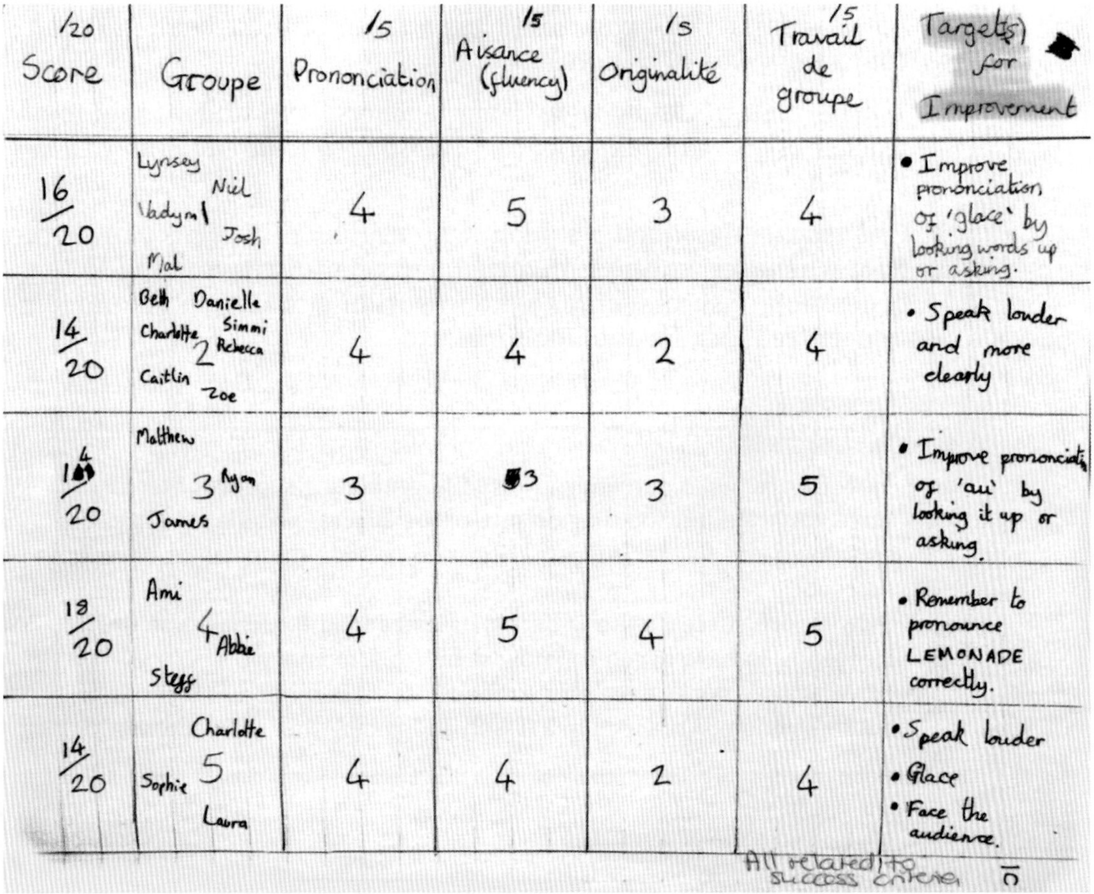

/20 Score	Groupe	/5 Prononciation	/5 Aisance (fluency)	/5 Originalité	/5 Travail de groupe	Targets for Improvement
16/20	Lynsey Niel Ladyml Josh Mal	4	5	3	4	• Improve prononciation of 'glace' by looking words up or asking.
14/20	Beth Danielle Charlotte Simmi 2 Rebecca Caitlin Zoe	4	4	2	4	• Speak louder and more clearly
14/20	Matthew 3 Ryan James	3	3	3	5	• Improve prononciati of 'au' by looking it up or asking.
18/20	Ami 4 Abbie Steff	4	5	4	5	• Remember to pronounce LEMONADE correctly.
14/20	Charlotte 5 Sophie Laura	4	4	2	4	• Speak louder • Glace • Face the audience.

All related to success criteria   5̄

Fig. 8.12 Pupil-generated peer-assessment grid

Impact – *as above, plus:*

- All students were aware of their achievement and were therefore more interested in what they were learning rather than 'who's the best in the class'.

- Students are more reflective about whether their strategies will meet learning objectives.

- There is a noticeable culture change in many classrooms, as control has shifted from teacher to student and learning has become more active.

- Students are better at checking and showing their working in mathematics.

- Success criteria have helped with differentiation, because students can instantly identify what is causing their particular difficulties.

- Teachers from the schools in all the teams said there had been a positive impact on exam results as a result of success criteria, and coursework was of a higher quality.

- Teachers felt that they were better teachers. One student said to a teacher of 16 years' experience, *'English used to be crap with you, but it's all right now!'*

- One teacher described a student who usually throws his pen on the floor whenever writing is involved, but after discussion and generation of success criteria, he was willing to have a go and joined in peer feedback for the first time.

Reflection

- How far are pupils currently involved in generating success criteria?
- Have you tried just focusing on one of the success criteria, and breaking that down into further success criteria to provide the detail to help pupils succeed?
- How far are success criteria becoming embedded (i.e. pupils use them frequently so have begun to know them from memory)?
- How far have pupils been able to modify success criteria as a result of putting them into practice in a lesson and finding they need altering?

9 How will we know what excellence looks like?

❝ Teacher: 'What helps you learn the best?'
Pupils: 'Seeing other pupils' work at the beginning of lessons. ❞
    Unanimous class vote, from Birmingham Learning Team teacher

Using success criteria has enabled pupils to have a sense of what their work should include, and, if success criteria are broken down and include examples along the way (see pages 111, 146), quality will be increased. Having, for any lesson, **one piece of work or product** from a previous class, which can be analysed by pupils at the beginning of a lesson or series of lessons, leads to:

- an understanding of the overall expectation, how the finished piece might look, how long it is, what exactly is meant by the learning objective in this context;

- through talk-partner discussion, the identification of success criteria – what the piece or product consists of;

- some indication of quality, as opinions are given by pupils about the impact of the work or skill shown.

Having, however, **two examples of differing quality side by side**, which can be compared and analysed by the class, leads to a more explicit and deeper understanding of quality, because:

- seeing *why* one example is more successful than the other, against specific success criteria, allows pupils to see what excellence looks like in real terms;

- seeing what one example includes, compared to what the other example does *not* include, communicates excellence much more explicitly than an example which simply shows good work: pupils see the impact of *not* using the relevant success criterion effectively on the quality of the whole piece of work, action, finished art or whatever.

This chapter outlines how teachers have been able to help pupils define and then use their understanding of quality in their own work, by a process of projecting and analysing old products of any form.

Comparing products to define quality

One of the most effective teacher resources is an ever-growing bank of old pieces of work or products, such as photographs of artwork or DT models, video snapshots of PE or games, examples of pupil writing in any subject, or mathematics. These can be used at the beginnings of lessons, or series of lessons, for a variety of purposes, all of which involve pupils instantly in the process of learning.

By using these examples for analysis through talk-partner discussion, pupils are actively engaged in seeing what is expected in its finished form, determining success criteria and – if two examples are being compared – identifying quality. Rather than beginning lessons by teacher input or teacher–pupil question and answer, pupils in classes led by learning team teachers now start each lesson immersed in thinking and analysing, within the parameters of the learning objective and context, before they begin any independent work.

This has led to a better balance: teachers have in the past done too much work, with too few pupils actively involved during the critical setting-up stage of lessons, and with some pupils often opting out because the teaching style has allowed this. *All* pupils have to be involved if they are immediately asked to decide, in talk partners, what they can see in this example or – if there are two – what exactly makes this one better than that one, linking their analysis to success criteria.

Another breakthrough has been the fact that pupils are now more often seeing completed pieces of work *before* they do it themselves, rather than after they have finished. It seems ludicrous now to believe that it was supposed to be helpful to have a plenary showing excellent work *after* pupils had finished – too late for them to go back and start again. We now know that showing the best work at the beginning of a lesson or series of lessons has a significant impact on pupil confidence in understanding expectations and demonstrating excellence.

The underlying reluctance of teachers to do this has been their fear that rife copying would ensue. Nothing could be further from the truth. Across all fourteen learning teams, only a minority of pupils have copied from such examples – and that amounted to higher quality work than those pupils would have produced independently, by giving them models, words, and so on, which they could then internalise and make their own. Using other pupils' previous work to analyse in this way inspires and challenges pupils to do better.

Emma Bradshaw, from the Essex Learning Team, provides an example of using this technique for a handwriting lesson: more examples, across the age range, follow.

HANDWRITING LESSON

Learning objective: To know what makes a good piece of handwriting

Context: Comparing two pieces of handwriting from SAT mark scheme

Two handwriting samples from the QCA national tests Writing mark schemes were scanned into the interactive whiteboard. Talk partners discussed the 'good' and 'bad' bits of each, and then shared ideas as a class and annotated the samples. The success criteria for children's own handwriting were drawn up using the ideas collected and added to, with some points relating directly to the handwriting style taught in Emma's school. Both samples are shown in Fig. 9.1, with annotations by pupils.

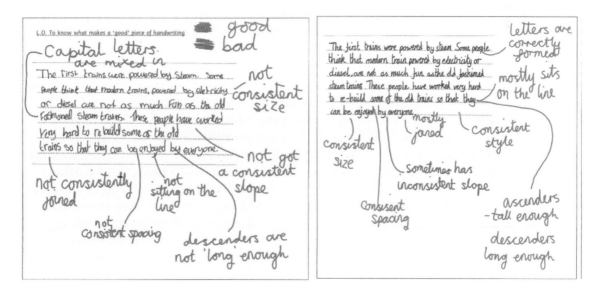

Fig. 9.1 Handwriting samples

Success criteria generated by the pupils as a result of this comparison:

- Form each letter correctly
- Make sure letters are a consistent size
- Join all the letters except capitals Q, Z, X
- 'Loop' the letters g, y, f, j
- Make ascenders tall enough and descenders long enough
- Use consistent spacing
- Sit the letters on the line
- Write with a consistent slope
- Write in a consistent style

What teachers have learnt about comparison analyses

There are some useful practical tips which teachers have learned to maximise the success of this technique:

1   The younger the children, the bigger the quality gap needs to be between the two examples – otherwise, the difference are too subtle for a worthwhile comparison to take place.

2   The older the pupils, the smaller the quality gap can be (some teachers like to use *three* pieces for analysis).

3   The two pieces **must be anonymous**. Taking two pieces *from the class* and discussing publicly which is better and why the other falls down would be insensitive in the extreme. This is not to say that **one piece** should never be taken from within the class and discussed by the class – in fact the next chapter goes on to describe how effective it can be to stop lessons, project **one child's work** chosen at random, and have the class analyse it against the success criteria. (When *anyone's* work can be chosen for a mid-lesson analysis, everyone is happy to have their work displayed, so **random selections** are vital in enabling all children to feel confident – in fact thrilled – to have their work discussed.) Formative assessment is an ipsative process: you are always trying to compete against yourself and improve your own previous performance, so having successes and improvement pointed out in your work is welcome. Being compared to another class member, however, where you come off badly, is the quickest way to reinforce a fixed mindset of *'I must be no good at this'*.

4   If the learning objective is related to a creative aspect of the subject (e.g. descriptive writing/ending a story), there is a danger that pupils will believe that the two examples shown are the *only* ways of fulfilling the success criteria. It is therefore important to make available other

examples of the same success criteria being fulfilled, but in different ways (not necessarily for close analysis, just to make the point). It is also necessary to be explicit about other possibilities, so that pupils do not feel confined to the examples given.

5   Increasingly, teachers are storing examples of products electronically, removing the need for elaborate filing and overcoming the problem of how to project them. Using a split screen means pieces can be projected side by side.

6   Projecting old pieces of written work at the beginning of a lesson can be a problem if the technology is unavailable. Some people photocopy the pieces; some scan them into their computer and project them on the interactive whiteboard. Photographs can be projected in the same way. However, the most effective analysis and discussion takes place when pupils can see the two examples side by side. For this, the best device available appears to be a *Visualiser*. A visualiser is a video camera on a stand which will project anything laid underneath it as a live, moving image. Visualisers have provided the technical answer for projecting work, so we can now do something we have never before been able to do: analyse pieces of work which were too small for everyone to see at once.

7   Having enough samples of old pieces of contrasting work can be a problem if this collection has only just begun. Some strategies:

- Old pieces can be 'acquired' from parallel or similar-age classes, another school, online resources or, if desperate, can be made up by the teacher. When the examples used are necessarily brief (e.g. good or not-so-good similes), it is clearly easier for the teacher to make up the examples.

- Many teachers show one example from a previous class and use something the teacher deliberately did badly as the inferior example, openly admitting that this is their own work. If two contrasting pieces cannot be found, this works well and causes great hilarity. However, very young children sometimes assume that the best piece must, of course, be the teacher's – even when presented with obvious rubbish!

- Examples from texts are often used, but, where pupils' work has been used instead, there is greater interest, even fascination, more engagement and a credibility factor which cannot be underestimated. If pupils see that someone from this school could produce this standard, they believe they can do it themselves – maybe even better. Analysing the work of a known author, or the work of a teacher, is a process which can have a reverse effect.

The impact of analysing two products can be summarised for all age groups:

As a result of comparing two products:
- Higher standards are promoted and expectations raised, so pupils produce higher quality work, a wider vocabulary, etc.
- Pupils learn to justify their opinions.
- Pupils are motivated to work and don't worry about expectations.
- Plenaries are now about 'where to next' rather than showing examples of good work.
- Success criteria become embedded more quickly.
- Problems are pre-empted by showing them in the poorer piece.
- More is being covered and achieved in less time.
- Pupils can determine the improvements that are needed to get from one stage to another, rather than simply being told how to improve their own work.
- Pupils are inspired to be creative rather than to copy.
- Secondary students can improve their exam results by analysing previous exam attempts.

In the following examples of practice across the age ranges, there are many references to the types of comparisons which might be made, and two full examples where we can see every stage of a lesson, including the finished work as a result of the process.

Examples of use and impact of comparing products

Nursery/Reception (3, 4 and 5 year olds)

▸ Self-portraits (see Fig. 9.2 for examples), good and bad singing, good and bad playing of musical instruments, robot building.

▸ In one nursery, the teacher compared her own poor painting of an apple with the nursery nurse's beautiful picture. The children were asked how they could help the teacher improve her work; they generated the success criteria and then talked about the criteria as they did their own painting. Children aged 3–5 were able to discuss their work and demonstrated a pride in what they were doing. They were able to succeed against their own success criteria.

Fig. 9.2 Self-portraits

Years 1 and 2 (6 and 7 year olds)

▸ A simple leaf drawing and a detailed leaf drawing (see Fig. 9.3); instructional writing; good and bad balance in PE (the teacher asked a high achiever to 'do it wrong' compared to someone else doing it well).

Fig. 9.3 Leaf drawings

> ▸ An interesting example: one piece of writing had lots of connectives while the other repeated 'and' lots of times. The longer piece was the poorer piece in terms of connectives, yet the class thought it must be better because there was more writing. This showed the teacher what seemed to matter to them as a definition of quality.

Years 3 and 4 (8 and 9 year olds)

> ▸ Photographs of good and bad tennis grips and feet position; Egyptian war paintings; two bar graphs; letter writing; video of speaking and listening; simile poems; two addition sums; good and bad complex sentences; a smudgy charcoal drawing and a good one.

> ▸ One teacher showed levelled writing across four National Curriculum levels which led to higher-level writing than before.

Years 5 and 6 (10 and 11 year olds)

> ▸ It was very useful to compare Year 6 with Year 4 stories, which led to the generation of 'advanced' success criteria.

> ▸ One teacher had a class for a second year running, so was able to show one pupil's work compared to his work a year before for the same learning objective.

> ▸ Younger pupils' work was used to compare with the Year 5 example. Pupils in the Year 5 class were very careful to avoid making the same mistakes the younger pupil had made.

> ▸ Two Design Technology picture frames; good and not-so-good conclusions; good and excellent writing; tired imagery in a poem, compared to effective imagery; writing planning; research; handwriting; two pieces of science writing, one with correct vocabulary.

> ▸ Because of the subjective nature of art, it is better to confine this technique to the use of specific art techniques and how well a particular mood or effect had been created.

> ▸ One teacher showed the class a good and not-so-good letter and had signed the poorer letter herself. The class immediately assumed that her letter must be best!

> ▸ Cath Ayles, a junior school teacher, describes the impact of using this approach with her Year 5 class:

Learning objective: To write from someone's point of view

Context: The poem 'The Highwayman'

At the end of a two-week project on *The Highwayman* poem, Cath began by showing the pupils the 'not so good' example of work from last year's class. The pupils came up with several reasons for this not being so good, such as no adjectives or extended sentences. They were then shown the good example (see Fig. 9.4 for both examples) and, with their talk partner, came up with lots of good features which became the pupil-generated success criteria. The pupils then began their own writing.

The Highwayman

I went up to the pub door on my horse. I was singing to Bess. She opened the window and said hi. I said I was going to rob some gold for her. I left her and went to the highway and hid in a bush. I wanted to rob lots of people to get some gold. Two men came past me and I robbed them. I got their watches, some money and a gold chain. Bess will be happy with me. I went back to the pub but I went over the hill and saw Bess tied to a barrel dead. I was really sad. I went back to the highway. Then someone shot me.

The Highwayman

I was riding down the highway thinking about beautiful Bess. The horses' hooves clip clopped along the dusty track leading up to the pub. I reached the window. The shutters were all shut tight so I started to sing. The tune was sweet but loud enough for Bess to hear. She appeared at the window, her black shiny hair resting on her shoulders and a smile as bright as the sun. She was clearly pleased to see me. I held her hand and promised to bring her some gold. Suddenly, I heard a noise coming from the barn next door. I looked round, startled, but there was nothing there (probably just a small animal scurrying for food). I kissed Bess and was away into the darkness.

I returned to the highway and found a suitable place to hide out. It was a slow night and I did not see anyone until the early hours of the morning. There were two young men, on their way to work I imagine. I jumped out in front of them and got their watches, some money and a lovely gold chain without any bother at all. They gave them to me and continued on their journey without a word. Although I had promised Bess I would be back because work had been so slow I thought I owed Bess more gold so I stayed out another night. Unfortunately there were no more people walking down the highway (I think rumours may have spread about me working here!) so I went back to the pub to be with Bess.

I went as fast as I could up the road and just over the brow of the hill I could see the pub in the distance. By there was something outside the door. I got closer and stopped dead in my tracks. There was blood all over the floor and Bess was tied to a barrel. My jaw dropped open and my eyes welled up. My beautiful Bess what had they done to her.

I turned round and galloped away, I had to get away. I pictured Bess in my head, I remembered holding her hand, I could still smell her perfume on my collar, my tears rolled down my face and ....

Fig. 9.4 *The Highwayman* examples

Cath tells the rest of the story:

'At the end of the lesson, one of my Teaching Assistants who works with a statemented child came up to me with James's work. It brought a tear to my eye! I could not believe his achievements. He had taken some of the ideas, but then added to them and extended them to make them even better. My TA had not prompted him, said it was all his own work and he had only asked for a few spellings.

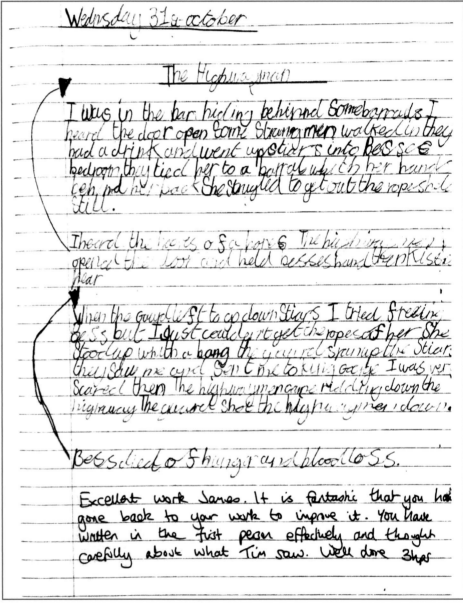

Fig. 9.5 James's writing

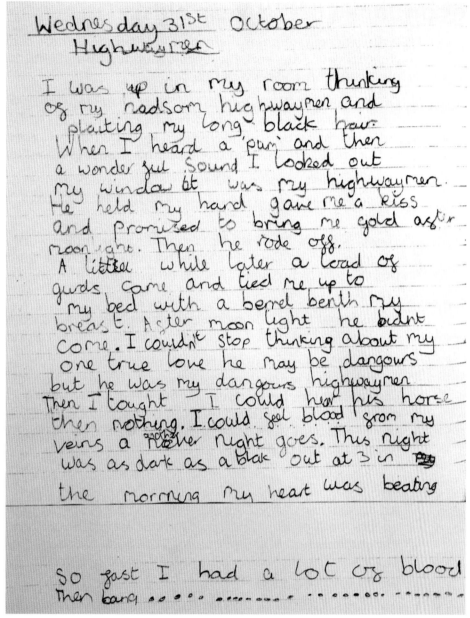

Fig. 9.6 Another low-achiever's work

'When I marked the rest of the work I found a similar effect. Some of the children had used the ideas but not all of them. Some didn't use any but knew how to set out the work and make it effective. The standard of work from that lesson was unbelievable. I am using this technique now in other subjects and everyone on the staff is excited by the examples we are sharing.'

Secondary (12–18 year olds)

▸ If the teacher generates the two products there is more copying, whereas when the work has been generated by students, it seems to make students feel they can do better.

▸ One teacher described how a Key Stage 4 student was concerned about the quantity of his work, but, when he compared his work with the best piece he could see that his own work met the success criteria and at least matched the quality, despite his anxieties about length.

▸ Many teachers showed students levelled answers from exams and asked, for instance, *'What could you do to make this Level 7 response Level 8?'*

▸ Teachers decided that students should not be shown work which was too many levels above their own, because it would be unattainable. It was thought to be useful to show *extracts* of A* thinking and build up from there.

▸ It was found in an all-age special school that it was more successful to analyse just one piece of work, as students' attention wandered.

▸ One teacher showed students three pieces of work at different levels after they had made their first attempt. This led to dissatisfaction and one student tore his work up, saying *'What I have written is rubbish. I'm going to start again.'* This reinforced the fact that students need to be shown excellent work *before* they begin their own, so that they are better informed and equipped.

Art

▸ An art teacher showed the students two charcoal drawings of different quality, both of which had met the success criteria for technical skill. The students had different opinions of which was better and why. There was free discussion and students were able to talk about what makes a stylistic difference.

▸ Another art teacher found it successful to model wrong and right ways of using certain skills by showing the students herself (e.g. how not to construct a clay pot) – which had been successful and fun!

PE

▸ One teacher taught an A-level lesson about the bio-mechanics of movement (all the forces that apply, like gravity or centrifugal force or pushing and pulling), focusing on high jumping. He displayed two photographs: one of an Olympic high jumper and another from the school sports day. The students were asked why one jump was more effective than the other in terms of forces, and through peer discussion were able to explain the differences between the bio-mechanical forces used. The impact was a greater use of technical terminology. Before this, they could either do the practical jump or explain about forces, but now they were able to apply the theory. *'If I had given them the task of writing why a school jumper could not do as well as an Olympic jumper, they would have struggled.'*

▸ Another PE teacher in a special school made the point that some pupils with autism or challenging behaviours are often skilled imitators, so care needs to be taken when demonstrating wrong ways of doing things.

Geography

▸ One teacher had saved last year's write-ups of a brook study and asked students to decide the level of each piece. This had led to them being able to improve their own work from the beginning.

Technology

▸ A technology teacher found comparing two products worked very well. The products range from hats to bags to electronic games. Some examples are stored while others are digitally photographed, but the real object is more powerful.

History

▸ One teacher had higher exam grades for his current cohort than for previous years – as a result, he believed, of the analysis of previous work being undertaken.

Mathematics

▸ As a matter of course now, one teacher shows the students one question answered well and one answered badly, from previous student work. Talk partners discuss points and generate the success criteria. After doing their own work, they swap and mark each other's work against the success criteria. The impact is that students now look for key vocabulary in the question and give more in-depth answers where explanations are required.

English

▸ When introducing a new genre, one teacher first asked talk partners to create success criteria from a good model of a recipe. The teacher then chose two students' work at random during the lesson and enlarged them to A3 size for the next lesson. Talk partners then chose two positive points and one to improve for each, then did the same with their own work.

▸ In Scotland, the SQA (Scottish Qualifications Authority) online pupil test answers, used in this way, had improved students' understanding of the exam requirements.

▸ One class was shown an example of a student's fire poster from last year and a published leaflet for comparison discussion. The resulting quality from all students was higher than for last year's students.

▸ An English teacher had used a previous class's film reviews for comparison to produce success criteria for a genre and look at the craft of writing. As a result, students were more aware of what was needed and produced the best film reviews this teacher had ever had. She also described how a particular series of lessons went wrong, but the students were able to unpick what had gone wrong via the success criteria.

▸ Melanie Watts, a high school teacher in Powys, gives a full example of an English lesson using this technique:

Learning objective: To understand how to and be able to write director's notes (Year 9, set 4 out of five)

Context: Romeo and Juliet – the fight scene (Act 3, Scene 1, lines 61–111)

Melanie began by giving the students one minute with talk partners to discuss the question *'What does the director of a play or film do?'* Answers were collected.

They then watched a short video clip of the fight scene. Students were encouraged to note facial expressions, movements, tone of voice, etc.

Two answers from previous students were projected on the OHP and students were given discussion time to decide which was better and why (see Fig. 9.7).

The students gave their response, generating the success criteria while doing so. The teacher annotated the 'best' piece as directed by the students. Melanie has found that keeping this copy of the annotated text visible, as well as the listed success criteria really helps students remember what each of the success criteria mean. Fig. 9.8 shows the annotated text. The final success criteria, in the students' own words, follow.

Tybalt: Romeo, the love I bear thee can afford
No better term that this-thou art a villain.

How to direct an actor -
Which piece of writing is better and why?

A. In this part of the scene Tybalt finally comes face to face with Romeo. This is the moment he has been waiting for since the Capulet party. He is furious and desperate to fight Romeo. Tybalt tries to start a fight by insulting him and by calling him a "villain".

B. Tybalt is still very angry because Romeo went to the Capulet party so he must pause before he says the words "thou art a villain". The words need to be said quietly so that only Romeo can hear but also slowly and deliberately with the greatest emphasis on the word "villain". Tybalt can stand very close to Romeo to make him feel threatened and uncomfortable. Tybalt's face needs to have a grim and determined look.

Fig. 9.7 Romeo and Juliet: previous work

how he is feeling   why he is feeling this way
Tybalt is still <u>very angry</u> because <u>Romeo went to</u>
where to pause
the <u>Capulet party</u> so he must <u>pause</u> before he

says the words "thou art a villain". The words
how to speak the lines
need to be said <u>quietly</u> so that only Romeo can
how to speak the lines
hear but also <u>slowly and</u> <u>deliberately</u> with <u>the</u>
how to speak the lines
<u>greatest emphasis on the word</u> "villain". <u>Tybalt</u>
movements and actions
<u>can stand very close to Romeo</u> to make him feel

threatened and uncomfortable. <u>Tybalt's face</u>
facial expression
<u>needs to have a grim and determined look.</u>

Fig. 9.8 Romeo and Juliet: annotated text

Director's notes – success criteria:

Give advice to the actor on:

- The way that they need to say their lines, e.g. shouting, whispering, where to pause
- Facial expressions
- The tone of voice that they need to use
- The movements and actions they should make and why
- What they are thinking and feeling and why

Students then discussed their task ready for the next lesson, in which they wrote their own directors' notes, peer-assessed them against the success criteria and developed them further.

Melanie: 'The impact of this approach on their work was quite pronounced as the quality of the work was so much better and much more focused – they did actually understand that they needed to "tell" the actors how to act out the scene. Also, while they were actually producing the work, there was less fussing and complaints of "I don't know how to do this."'

Reflection

- Do your pupils seem unsure about the 'big picture' of expectation – what the final product might look like?
- Do they often ask for reassurance?
- Have you kept examples of products from previous years? If not, how could you find ways of acquiring examples?
- Is your own or a colleague's concern about copying affecting pupils' ability to see excellence before they start their own work?

How can we enable a process of constant review and improvement?

6 *My work's not as neat today, but it sounds better.* 9

Eight-year-old

Chapter 8 dealt with learning objectives and success criteria as the tools with which we empower pupils to be come independent, active, reflective learners. Chapter 9 outlined the exciting outcomes of using analysis of old products before pupils start their own work, as a way of defining excellence and quality in real terms. This chapter focuses on the act of self-, peer- and teacher-evaluation of learning. Although the order of these chapters is logical, in the classroom they are not so rigidly defined, and, had it been possible, I would like to have combined them all into one chapter. Because each of these aspects has its own issues, I have dealt with them separately – and, in any case, a combined chapter would have amounted to half the book! This chapter, then, should be read as a continuation of all the previous chapters, because everything comes together at this point in a lesson: through the whole-lesson examples presented here you will see pupil analysis of old pieces of work, talk-partner discussion, pupil-generation of success criteria and self- and peer-evaluation during lessons and the teacher's place in marking.

As self- and peer-evaluation is considered now for the first time in depth, we need to explore the issues and establish current thinking and practice.

How feedback has evolved

When I first started working with teachers on formative assessment, in 1997, the main challenge for feedback was to improve teachers' marking. Marking was often focused on secretarial skills and comments were unhelpful (e.g. *'I really enjoyed reading this'*). There followed a period of more 'diagnostic' marking, where the 'success and improvement' approach developed with teachers in Surrey schools was used extensively to improve the feedback given to pupils. This became known as *'pinks and greens'* (tickled pink and green for growth), *'three stars and a wish'*, and other terms. This marking focused on the learning objective and increasingly, the success criteria. Although this was a great improvement, there were still problems:

- the marking was necessarily done away from the pupils, so the feedback was late and in a written form, sometimes hard to access;

- time had to be found for subsequent improvements to be made;

- marking all the books in this way was unmanageable for every lesson;

- many teachers still suggested how future work could be improved, in a different context – this is unhelpful, as pupils need to make the improvement on the *current* piece of work to be able to internalise and then apply the improvement needed to other contexts.

Self- and peer-evaluation began with rather crude ways of pupils deciding how well they were doing: traffic lights at the end of the work or other rating systems or, better, swapping work and marking for success and improvement, either alone or together. The problem with end-point evaluation is that it comes too late for any worthwhile improvement to be made. *Evaluation needs to be constant – as the learning is happening – so that changes can be made or new thinking applied* **while the work is in progress**, *rather than retrospectively.* Retrospective improvements are usually tinkering, whereas 'in progress' evaluation impacts the quality of the whole assignment.

Teachers in the learning teams began a natural process of trying to overcome these problems by attempting to integrate success and improvement through modelling and self- and peer-feedback into lessons. They found that pupils could fairly easily identify their own and each other's successes against success criteria, but deciding what could be improved – and then being able to make the improvements – was another, more difficult matter.

Finally, the breakthrough came with the use of the visualiser or any other technological device which enables a teacher to project one randomly chosen pupil's work part way through a lesson and use it for whole-class evaluation, deciding what was successful and what could be improved, then, in pairs, actually creating the improvement there and then for that person's work. The power of this 'on the spot' feedback meant that the rest of the class now had a highly contextualised model of what they might do to improve their own work, so their subsequent self- and peer-evaluation within the lesson of their own and their partner's work was, for the first time, successful for all learners – an excellent model of 'personalised learning'. There have now been two years of trialling, so we know both the impact of 'in-lesson' feedback and practical tips to make it work. These elements are described below, with examples across the age ranges.

What teachers have learnt about integrating feedback in lessons

▸ The pupil selected for whole-class success and improvement of their work must be randomly selected, perhaps by a 'draw' using named lollysticks, so that the message is clear: *anyone's* work can be identified for success and improvement. If pupils are selected by the teacher, they become anxious and demotivated about the process of analysis, whereas when it might be anyone, there is excitement about possibly being the one to be chosen.

▸ A visualiser (or other device) is essential for on-the-spot projection of work and there is no real substitute (reading it out doesn't work), although the following strategies are better than nothing:

● The pupil is chosen at random before they start work and works for that lesson on the laptop or on acetate for use with an overhead projector.

● A 'flexi-cam' is used – smaller and less robust and effective than a visualiser, but much cheaper.

● The work is scanned-in and projected via the interactive whiteboard.

● The work is quickly photocopied by a teaching assistant and given out for pairs to analyse with the teacher.

● For very short pieces of writing, the work can be enlarged to A3 so that the whole class can read it.

● Art can be seen by everyone if it is large enough.

● The randomly selected pupil works at the whiteboard.

● If the focus is short, the random pupil's work is written up on the whiteboard (e.g. complex sentence/simile/calculation).

● In some secondary schools, a random student's work is typed up for the next lesson.

▸ I have been astonished at the passion with which teachers have reported to me the impact of using a visualiser, so I include two such reports here. The first is an email I received, and the second some examples of pupil comments about how the visualiser has transformed their mathematics lessons.

Glenys Bradshaw, a junior school teacher, emailed me:

'The biggest impact of all has developed since I returned to the school with stories of visualisers. Within a matter of months all 16 classes in our school have their own. I cannot stress enough the impact that these have had. I have used it in lessons across the whole curriculum having mini-plenaries throughout. Being able to show children's work and edit it throughout the lesson and making improvements has been a big incentive for improvement for everyone. They are desperate to have their work shown! I have also used it during our rocks and soil topic, splitting the screen and showing a rock on one half and magnifying it on the other. I have never had such good quality work before.'

Nick Craven, a high school teacher in Moray, sets the class a task – a calculation or problem – collects in the books there and then, and randomly picks two or three people's work and projects it on the screen. He has bags of named lollysticks for each class, so the random selection is clear. Talk partners discuss the methods used for success and improvement, and class discussion with the teacher then follows. Typical prompts Nick uses are:

'Does your work look like this?'
'Is it better?'
'What could you do to make it better?'
'Have you done the same thing, but differently?'

Student comments (all were in this vein – the only negative comment from one student was that the lighting could have been better!):

S5 and S6 (lower and upper sixth, comparable to AS level):
'Allows comparison of work and allows pupils to see different methods of working mathematical problems out and shows good and bad points of the different methods. Also adds more interest to the lesson because pupils feel more involved with the lesson because their work is on screen.'

'I think that the projector thing is OK because it lets you see how people have worked out their work, helping you understand sometimes things you don't fully understand'.

'It makes me carry out full working now.'

'Nice to see pupils' work, not just the teacher's.'

'Really good as it saves time as examples don't need to be written out on the board. It also improves presentation of work.'

Younger students (set 5 of five):
'I think it is good if it is up on the screen because if you make mistakes people in the class can correct your answer.'

'People learn different methods from the book that is up on the screen'.

'I like seeing my work up on the board. It helps me understand the work and see the mistakes that I make.'

▸ To facilitate self- and peer-marking, pupils' books are more effectively used if pupils only do their work on the right-hand page, with the left side available for improvements, edit notes, peer comments, etc, to be made. This creates more space and stops work looking overcrowded and messy.

▸ Children from special schools often need this process to be developed one-to-one.

▸ With very young children it is more effective to analyse anonymous pieces of work first in a group setting until they understand how the process works, then to analyse one child's work at random. It is also important to make sure the first focus is on what is *good* about the piece, or children can see the process as negative and a signal that their work is not good enough.

▸ After a while, teachers gradually get to know instinctively where in the lesson to stop to project work

▸ 'Success' needs to be focused on *where the skill has been done the best, not just included.* By emphasising the very best examples of practice, pupils learn how to make their own improvements.

▸ Pieces should be assessed, not only for aspects of success and improvement needs, but should also be viewed holistically, as sometimes there are, for instance, words, phrases, certain flair or flow which make the work 'more than the sum of its parts'. Similarly, the individual success criteria might be brilliantly met when viewed in isolation, but the finished piece might lack the overall 'wow' factor when considered holistically. This is an important discussion to have with pupils. No matter how good the successes and improvements are, it is the impact of the whole, finished product which matters in the end. Also, as previously stated, the more different versions of excellence encountered, the greater will be the 'nose for quality' developed by pupils.

Word of warning: one inspector complained about the lack of marking by a teacher since using this approach. This teacher had not been writing anything at all on their books – which is inadvisable. A short acknowledgment comment seems best, but checking pupil work for future planning is vital. This incident brought up the importance of having a whole-school policy for what is and what is not teacher-marked, and the need for possible codes for peer-marking, oral marking and so on.

The impact of integrated self- and peer-evaluation can be summarised for all ages:

- The random selection of the work for class analysis leads to a high level of focus, as pupils have no idea if they might have to show their work!
- Pupils are excited by the prospect and welcome the opportunity to have their work 'marked' or commented on by the class, with both success and improvement needs discussed and improvements made.
- Subsequent finished work is of higher quality than work done without this process: more quality, less quantity and, by the end of a lesson, everyone's work has improved.
- As with all aspects of formative assessment, because learning is more engaging, pupils are better behaved.
- Boys work noticeably harder and raise their achievement. Teachers believe this is because of the short focus of tasks and the need to make sure their work is good enough for public display!
- Increasingly, pupils can't help themselves editing their own work as one person's work is being analysed. This can be a problem, as teachers need pupils' full attention.
- The process has moved the plenary from the end to the beginning and throughout the lesson. Plenaries at the end simply reinforced pupil inadequacy.
- The peer-marking follow-up to whole-class analysis has developed pupil confidence in the power and necessity of peer consultation and made them skilled at providing constructive criticism. Pupils seem more interested in peer comments than teacher comments.
- If a pupil has gone off in the wrong direction in their work, this process allows a chance to refocus and get back on track.
- Fewer children need reassurance, because they know they will be given time and the means to put things right.
- Lessons become shorter, as more is being achieved in a shorter time.
- Visually impaired pupils are, for the first time, seeing good examples of handwriting because of the visualiser, so their handwriting has improved.
- The teacher's role in marking is now to evaluate the quality of pupils' improvements in the light of future planning, making only minimal comments on the work, because the meaningful feedback has already taken place, so teachers are marking less. *Where teachers still mark in depth, it is more effective to do this for pieces of work in which skills are applied or brought together. Pausing lessons to model success and improvement will interrupt pupils unnecessarily if their work is a 'big' application task.*

Examples of integrated feedback

▸ Sally Hunter, an infant school teacher in the Wokingham Learning Team, describes two English lessons with her Year 2 class in which integrated feedback took place:

'I have found this very powerful for all the children in the class – higher and lower achievers. The quality of work has improved significantly and children can see where to make improvements in their own work rather than me telling them.'

LESSON I

Learning objective: To write powerful descriptive sentences

Context: An Autumn Walk

Children were first asked to tell their talk partner five things they could see in the picture (Fig. 10.1).

Fig. 10.1 An autumn walk

Feedback generated:

- *Lots of different coloured leaves*
- *A big tree near the front*
- *A dark hole*
- *Yellow, red, green, brown, orange*
- *Leaves all over the ground*

Sally showed the class three good sentences and they discussed what was good about them. Those features were underlined (Fig. 10.2).

The low branches are filled with crisp golden leaves which are dangling ready to fall to the ground.

Golden yellow leaves cover the ground like an autumn carpet.

Golden yellow leaves cover the ground and crunch under foot as children run past.

We started by looking at three good sentences. Children asked what was successful about them, what make them good sentences.

Fig. 10.2 Analysed sentences

Success criteria were generated by the children as a result of their analysis, as follows:

Remember to:
- Use describing words
- Use interesting, exciting, 'wow' words,
- Add detail

After about 15 minutes' writing, the work shown in Fig. 10.3 was chosen at random (using named lollysticks) and typed onto the smart board. Pairs decided three best bits and one place to improve. They decided the last sentence should not end with '*path*' and extended it.

The pupils then peer-evaluated their own work for best successes and improvements. One child's peer-discussed work is shown in Fig. 10.4. *Gracefully, Autumn carpet* and *bare* have been chosen as the 'best bits' and *brown woods* to be improved. The child has replaced that with *gloomy* and *spooky*.

The golden orange leaves fall from the different kinds of trees like oak and chestnut.

In Autumn the leaves change colour.

In October the yellow, red and orange leaves flutter to the soft ground.

The multi coloured leaves bend over to make a shady path

which, leads to the dark gloomy woods.

After about 15 minutes working, this work was produced by a child in the class. The child was randomly selected using lolly sticks and I typed it onto board for who class to feedback against the success criteria: pink and green. The improvement was not ending the sentence with path and adding 'which leads to the dark, gloomy woods.' Children then worked with talking partner to 'tickled pink and green for growth' their own work.

Fig. 10.3 One pupil's work, chosen at random and marked by the class

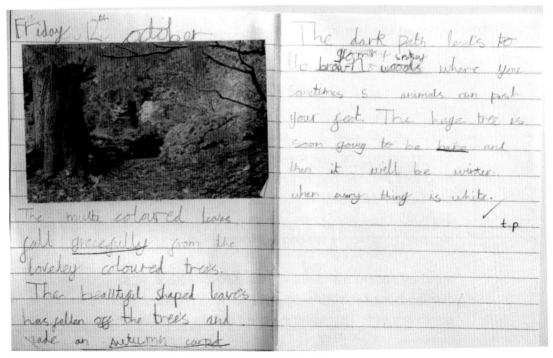

Fig. 10.4 A child's finished work

LESSON 2

Learning objective: To edit and improve our own work and to retell a story

Context: The story of Grace Darling

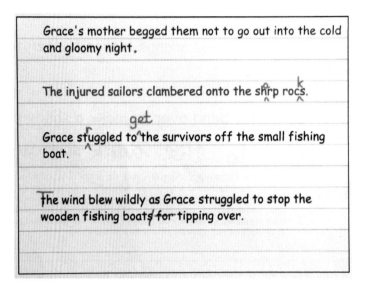

Fig. 10.5 Annotated sentences

Sally began the lesson by showing the pupils four sentences. Pairs had to decide what was wrong with each sentence (see Fig. 10.5).

With talk partners, pupils discussed a piece of work by a pupil in a previous class (Fig. 10.6) and, from that, generated the success criteria.

> She struggled to row the boat back to the lighthouse because the wind was blowing against her. After what felt like ages, Grace and her father spotted the red and white stripes of the lighthouse. Through the spray from the sea, Grace could barely see her mother frantically waving her arms.
>
> As they reached the rocks, they fought hard to stop the small fishing boat from tipping over. Gradually they began to help the survivors off. The sailors were freezing, wet and groaning in pain.

Fig. 10.6 Previous pupil's work used to generate success criteria

Success criteria were generated by the pupils as a result of their analysis, as follows:

Remember to:
- Use joining words: *and, because*
- Use describing words like *tall, rough*
- Write the things that happened in order
- Add lots of detail

One pupil's work (randomly chosen) was projected after 10–15 minutes and pairs decided 'pinks and green' for the piece, adding the word *tall* for the lighthouse (Fig. 10.7).

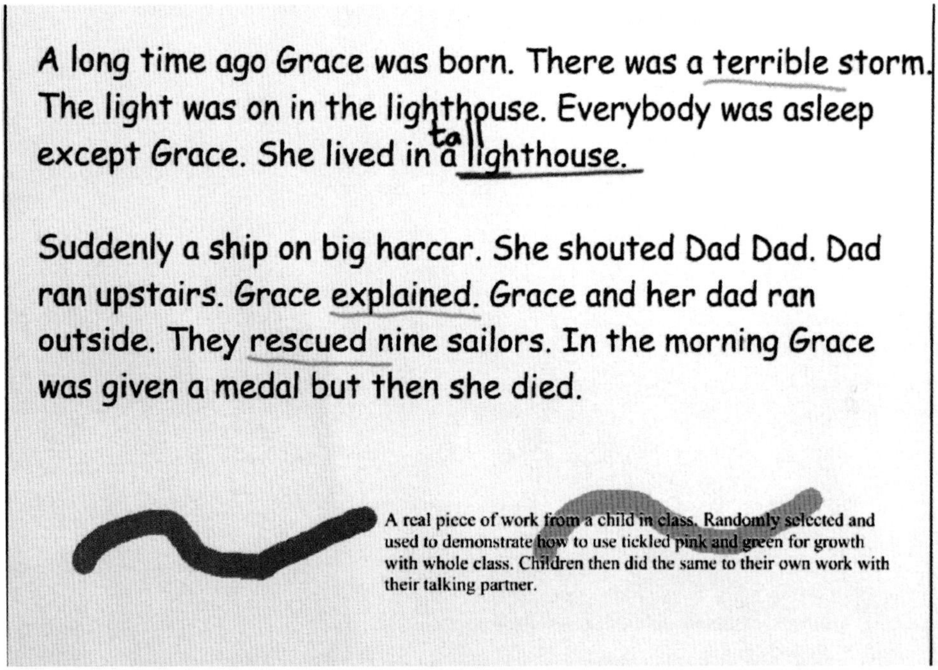

A long time ago Grace was born. There was a terrible storm. The light was on in the lighthouse. Everybody was asleep except Grace. She lived in a tall lighthouse.

Suddenly a ship on big harcar. She shouted Dad Dad. Dad ran upstairs. Grace explained. Grace and her dad ran outside. They rescued nine sailors. In the morning Grace was given a medal but then she died.

A real piece of work from a child in class. Randomly selected and used to demonstrate how to use tickled pink and green for growth with whole class. Children then did the same to their own work with their talking partner.

Fig. 10.7 One pupil's randomly chosen work, marked by the class

Pupils then peer-marked their work, working together on each other's writing: one example is shown (see Figs 10.8a,b). *Ginormous, horrible, jagged, very tired, petrified and climbed* were identified as 'best bits' and the word *rolling* was inserted to describe the waves.

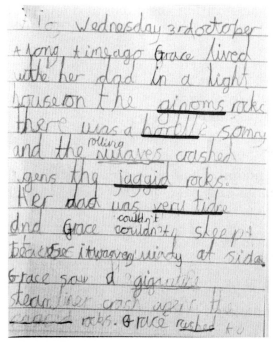

Fig. 10.8a Peer-marked work: page 1

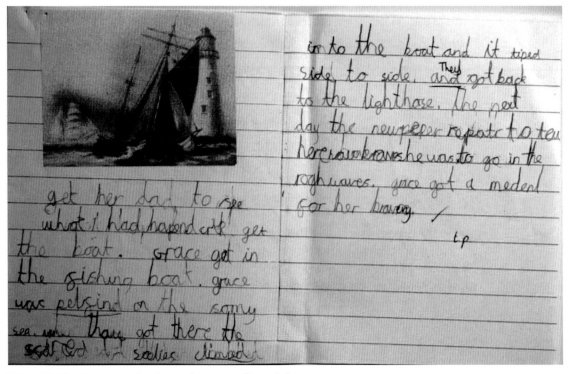

Fig. 10.8b Peer-marked work: pages 2 and 3

A long time ago Grace lived withe her dad in a lighthouse on the ginoms rocks. There was a horblle somry and the waves crashed igens the jaggid rocks. Her dad was very tidre and Grace couldn't sleep because it was very windy at side. Grace saw a gigantic steam liner crash agens the jaggid rocks. Grace rushed to get her dad to se what had hapend and get the boat. Grace got in the fishing boat. grace was pelfind on the somy sea. When thay got there the scared salies climbed in to the boat and it tiped side to side. and got back to the lighthouse. The next day the newpeper repatr told here how brave she was to go in the rogh waves. grace got a medenl for her bravre.

▸ Another English lesson follows, from Emma Bradshaw's Year 6 class:

Learning objective: To write poetry using personification, alliteration and simile

Context: War poems

The lesson began with talk partners analysing a previous Year 6 pupil's war poem. Pupils were asked to look for effective use of personification, alliteration and simile. The class identified one improvement – the repetition of the same word on consecutive lines. Fig. 10.9 shows the analysed piece.

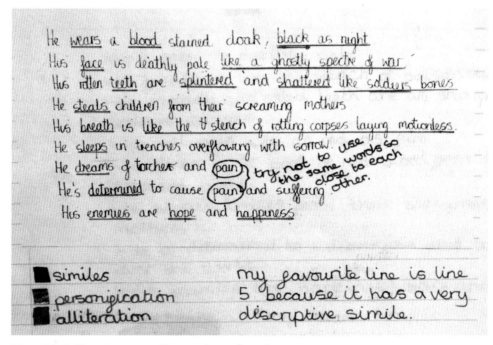

Fig. 10.9 Previous pupil's work analysed

Success criteria for the poem were then created from this analysis:

Success criteria:
- **Include images of war:**
  e.g. children screaming, weapons, dead soldiers, battlefields, etc.
- **Use vivid vocabulary:**
  e.g. *'deathly pale'* instead of *'white'*, *'splintered and shattered'* instead of *'broken'*.
- **Include poetical devices:**
  personification – describe war as if it is a human e.g. *'War wears . . .'*, *'War dreams of. . .'*, etc.
  simile – e.g. *'as black as night'* or *'like a ghostly spectre of war'*
  alliteration – e.g. *'hope and happiness'*

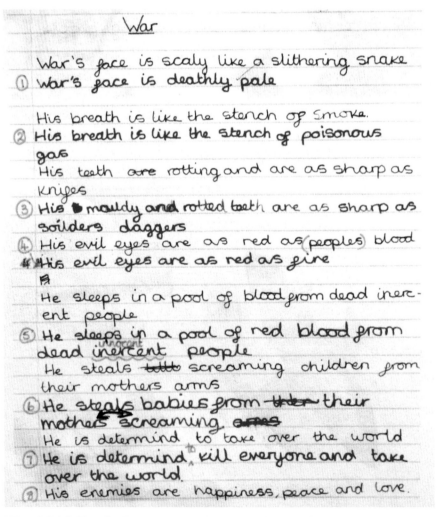

Fig. 10.10 Pupil's first draft, with peer-discussed revisions

Pupils then completed their first draft of their own poems, leaving room between each line for revisions. They discussed their poems with their partners throughout the lesson and wrote their improvement individually as a result underneath their first lines (see Fig. 10.10 for an example of first draft with numbered revisions underneath).

Pupils were then asked to complete their poems using the best ideas from original drafts and improvements (see Fig. 10.11 for the final draft).

Fig. 10.11 Pupil's final poem

▸ The last example is in the context of history, from a Salford high school teacher, Gary Day-Lewis.

1 In developing peer-assessment in the history department, as a means of raising achievement, Gary began by making sure that all learning objectives were clear. He then produced some *generic* success criteria for key skills used in history, for example:

Learning objective	Context	Success criteria
We are learning to understand how to produce a successful essay using sources to support our own conclusion	Was Oliver Cromwell a hero or a villain?	**Remember to:** • Produce a three-part essay, with introduction, middle and conclusion • Identify his successes and failures using primary source evidence • Produce a series of structured paragraphs with suitable topic sentences • Provide your own opinion, justified with supporting evidence

2   Students were then asked to peer-assess each other's work. They were given prompt cards to guide them in their assessments:

Topic sentences
Use some of the following comments in your assessments. . .
• I love this topic sentence!
• Try a different one from the wall display.
• Have you thought about using. . . ?
• Well done, each paragraph begins with a different topic sentence.
• Try to vary the wording of your topic sentences.
• Good choice of an opening sentence.
• What are you trying to introduce with this sentence?
• Your topic sentence should introduce the purpose of the paragraph.

Use of quotes
• Does the essay contain at least five quotes?
• Are they used correctly to support a fact or comment?
• Are they placed in correct speech marks?
• Are they included as part of a sentence?
• Do you think they are in the right place?
• Do they need to include more quotes?

3   Ground rules were established to ensure that peer-marking would provide a positive outcome for all students engaged.

4   In the next lesson, the class was divided into five groups of six, and each group was provided with two pieces of work taken from the previous year's essays – one good and one slightly below average. The students were then asked to discuss the work and mark them against the success criteria. They were then provided with the levelled marking scheme (below) and asked to reassess the pieces of work.

What your level means:
Level 2: *You have only given one or two events from Oliver Cromwell's reign as Lord Protector. You have not really explained your reason.*
Level 3: *You have given more than one event from Cromwell's reign, but we still need more reasons. Also, instead of just a list of reasons, we need the reasons to be explained more carefully.*
Level 4: *You have given quite a few events and decisions from Cromwell's reign. You have also explained most of your reasons.*
Level 5: *Your introduction is clear and accurate. You have given several reasons why you have chosen a number of events from Cromwell's reign. You have shown how some of the reasons/events are connected. You have also explained why you think that one reason/event is more important than the others.*
Level 6: *You have done the things described in Level 5, but your work is even more carefully planned and accurate. You have shown that you have looked at different pieces of evidence and that you understand why different people have different views about what happened.*
Level 7: *You have done all the things described above, but you have also shown that you are able to evaluate different points of view and that you can make your own judgements, based on suitable evidence.*

5   The students were very accurate in their judgements and did some more essay marking against the criteria.

6   For the next lesson, in the same groups, students were asked to assess their peers' essays. Students' pieces were unnamed, having a three-digit code to ensure no friendship biasing (or the opposite). Each student was given one essay to assess, and had to mark against the success criteria until three minutes had passed. They then had to pass the essay clockwise to the next person in the group. This was repeated until all six essays had been assessed and comments added to each. Fig. 10.12 gives one example of a peer-marked essay.

In the subsequent feedback lesson, students were asked to complete a feedback sheet after looking at their returned essay, and to decide targets for improvement.

Oliver Cromwell – Hero or Villain

In this essay I am going to discus Oliver Cromwell's life and decide whether he was a villain or a hero.

A hero is a person who has exceptional courage and who fights for a cause.

A villain is a person who is wicked or evil. Someone who does evil deliberately.

[handwritten margin notes: This «is a popular say to start the essay- well done. great balance — should this he ...tor? — behaviour]

Oliver Cromwell was born on April 25, 1599, in Huntingdon. His family had very little property, but he wasn't classed as a commoner. In 1620 Oliver married Elizabeth Bourcheir and they started their married life with very little money. Cromwell's business failed in 1630, making him move to St.Ives to become a farmer. When his uncle died in 1637 Oliver inherited a modest income and property.

Cromwell was fortunate that his grandfather lived in a state house where royalty and court official often visited. Oliver had many opportunities to mix with these powerful figures and via his father-in-law he became in contact with leading puritan figures. By 1630 Cromwell underwent a religious conversion to the puritan cause and it was said that 'he was waiting for god to give him a mission'.

Oliver Cromwell was elected as a member of parliament for Huntingdon and he attended between 1628 -9, although he was probably the poorest MP there. By 1640 he was one of the most out spoken critics of royal policies, and it was his ambition for parliament (and not the king) to have the power.

In 1653 Cromwell had had enough of the greedy MPs who used the taxes to make themselves rich. The people were keen to have a king again and they asked Cromwell to take over this role but Cromwell refused. He did however agree to become Lord Protector, but his enemies said that he was greedy and had taken all the power of the king, without the title.

Cromwell died on 3rd September 1658. He was buried at Westminster Abbey. After Cromwell's death Charles II appeared

[handwritten margin note: could have use split into more paras.]

from exile and had Cromwell's body dug back up and hung at
Tyburn. Oliver's head was cut off and displayed for nearly twenty
years outside Westminster Hall.

I think that Oliver Cromwell genuinely tried his hardest to solve
the problems of the government at the time and he was aware of
the dishonesty and greed of the MPs. However Cromwell took
advantage of this and didn't quite make hero status.

is there anymore than sarcasm?

Some people thought Oliver Cromwell was a villain because when
Charles II (Son of Charles I) rebelled and trouble arose in Ireland
and Scotland Cromwell dealt with the situation in a ferocious
manner which earned him a reputation for cruelty.

Historians have made many references to Cromwell's behaviour
and many believed that he was "an inhuman monster." *- Good quote!*

good use of villain evidence.

He was a religious man and a puritan (a strong protestant).
Cromwell believed that he should punish all Catholics. When he
took his army (the new model army) to Ireland in 1649 there were
reports that the Catholic rebels tried to surrender, but Cromwell
showed no mercy and said "No Quarter" and killed them anyway!
Also Oliver Cromwell tried to control the way people lived by
closing theatres, stopping Christmas, banning may pole dancing
and shutting pubs.

Good connective

In conclusion I think that Oliver Cromwell was a villain due to his
religious beliefs. Cromwell took his religion too seriously and
because of this it made him very unpopular with the people.

Lord Clarendon stated ' He is so wicked that he is damned, for
which hell-fire is prepared, yet he had some qualities which have
cause the memory of some men in all ages to be celebrated; and he
will be looked upon as a brave, bad man'.

Could have used indents or missed a line to show paragraphs clearly!

great essay!

Well done. You started off the conclusion
with the correct phrase. You also included your opinion. Also, you have talked
about one event! ☺

No spelling mistakes ☺. No punctuational mistakes!

good essay!

Fantastic vicky!!

Some good connectives but you need to advance
them.

Brilliant essay! But you need to use more sources to
back up your opinions and evidence!

Fig. 10.12 Oliver Cromwell essay, peer-marked by six students

Gary summarises the impact of introducing formative assessment and, in particular, self- and peer-feedback:

'With the exception of a few individual pupils, initial wariness of the process soon gave way to enthusiasm, with pupils recognising the value of peer-assessment in developing their understanding of what made a successful outcome. The biggest challenge for me was to redevelop and rethink my role not as a teacher but as a facilitator. I found it a lot harder not to help pupils than to offer help when they ask for it or need it! Peer-assessment relies on pupils understanding and solving their own problems. Peer-assessment helped all my pupils to realise what they were doing wrong in their work, and helped them identify strengths or alternatives. One advantage that I had not previously considered was that it produced an element of competition which provided stimulus, especially for the boys: it provided the pressure to perform well, because it is embarrassing for somebody else to see your poor work, even if it is anonymous. There are also, of course, the very real benefits of instant feedback. Quick, even inaccurate feedback from peers has far more impact than slow and accurate feedback from a teacher.

'Pupil performance has improved significantly, with the number of Level 6 pieces of work in Year 8 increasing threefold from 3.6% to over 10%, but the most remarkable finding is that for many of the pupils marks no longer mattered. Standards of work improved as pupils were able to internalise and recognise the concept of good or not so good, and provide feedback. All the teachers involved in this have commented on time-savings.

'The pupils' comments were perceptive, positive and very useful – for example:

"I really liked the way that I now understand what the difference is between a Level 5 and a Level 6."

"I got a real buzz from reading what my mates thought of my work."

"It made me think about how much time and effort I should spend on my work if others are reading it."

'It has been one of the most liberating experiences of my teaching career to realise that the old notions of summative assessment could be counterproductive and that directed peer-assessment is so much more effective.

'Some pupils progressed from a Level 4 to Level 5 in their work in only three essays, which gave them the confidence they needed to develop still further in this subject.'

Reflection

- How much marking is done by you or teachers in your department/school?
- How far do you think it impacts pupil progress?
- Have you tried whole-class 'success and improvement' modelling with one pupil's piece in the middle of a lesson?
- Is there any technology available which could be used to project work mid-lesson?
- What would need to happen to enable self- and peer-assessment to be a necessary element of every lesson in your class/school?
- How far do pupils in your secondary classes/school understand, in precise terms, the difference between various levels?

11 Setting up a learning team in your own educational setting, and supporting teacher development

All the cultural and practical aspects of formative assessment have been thoroughly explored throughout this book, and illustrated by excellent examples of thinking and practice from teachers and their pupils in my one-year action research teams. The impact of teachers carrying out action research in their classrooms as a means of professional development cannot be understated. We have known for many years that 'cascading' or 'one teacher going on a course' are inadequate professional development models. Because of this awareness, a great deal of funding in the UK in recent years has been allocated to schools to encourage and support them to use action research as a model of staff development, within their own schools or within 'learning network communities'.

Over a period of seven years, running 44 teams, I have learnt so much about how to maximise the impact of action research learning teams, that I believe that detail can now be applied to any educational organisation wishing to embark on action research as a means of development. The first part of this chapter is an outline of the main elements involved in setting up a team – whether within a school, a group of schools, a college, a teachers' centre or any other educational setting. I also include, in this book, some helpful implementation advice from East Lothian and Gateshead authorities.

A very full descriptive account of exactly what needs to be done to follow the model of running an action research learning team – down to hiring hotel rooms, and so on – can be found on the *Active Learning through Formative Assessment* page on the Hodder Education website (www.hoddereducation.co.uk) and at www.shirleyclarke-education.org

The second part of this chapter is written by an Advanced Skills Teacher, Emma Goff, who was a member of the Tonbridge Learning Team and now works in Kent schools to help teachers make a positive impact on children's learning. She uses formative assessment as her key message, and her insights provide a useful complement to my description of an action research model. Whereas the learning-team model outlines practical and developmental issues, Emma describes the specific processes she uses to help teachers reflect on their practice and begin to take on formative assessment. In combination, the two provide a highly effective approach to raising pupil and teacher confidence, achievement and autonomy so that teachers and pupils become 'lifelong learners', applying their embedded skills to any new context.

1. Setting up an action research learning team

Establishing the aims of the project

Organisers first need to establish their vision for the impact of the project. Whether my teams are Local Authority-led or cluster group-led, they always want the same outcome: that as many schools as possible will ultimately benefit from the experience of the 30 members of the team, bringing formative assessment into *every* classroom for *every* teacher. It is therefore essential to decide what might be planned for the years following the one-year project. Some possible follow-ups – all of which, naturally, have funding implications – are:

1   The learning team reruns the showcase afternoon (a two-hour session at the end of the project) on a number of occasions to groups of schools, to stir up initial interest. The showcase is very powerful in doing this, because teachers hear real teachers talking about real children in very honest ways – what worked best, how they developed along the way, and so on. The message is always overwhelmingly enthusiastic and inspirational. The displays can be reused as a backcloth to any event.

2   A written summary of the impact of the action research is disseminated to all, with both qualitative and quantitative impact (i.e. anecdotal evidence, examples of pupil achievement and test results).

3   Key teachers from the learning team help run new learning teams, using the same model.

4   A new learning team is set up and each member is paired with an old learning team member, acting as a mentor, ideally spending some time working alongside each other.

5   Key teachers can be observed (or videoed) in their classrooms, demonstrating the various aspects of formative assessment.

The current learning team model

Thirty teachers form a team, in pairs from 15 schools, so that teachers have 'buddies' throughout the project. They meet me for three whole days during a calendar year: in January or February to start it off, in June to provide their first feedback, and in November for their last feedback and the showcase event in the afternoon. The calendar year is deliberate, because in the autumn term the teachers have a new context or class, so their findings are enriched by the 'new start' they make as a result of their learning so far. With more funding, four or five meeting days in the year would be ideal, in that there would be more time for the invaluable teacher discussion about the issues involved in their trialling, with other teachers from other schools. An interim twilight meeting is very supportive, between each of the days. Many coordinators also hold a heads' meeting, or introduce the project at a heads' meeting, to ensure that everyone is aware of the level of commitment needed in being involved in the project.

Regardless of funding, the number of teachers needs to be a maximum of 30, in order for discussion and feedback to fit into the time frame of a day and to maintain interest and motivation on the days. I have tried working with a larger group, with unsatisfactory results. It is very tempting to make the team bigger, assuming this will lead to the development of more experts, but the reverse is actually true.

There needs to be someone who will be able to provide *initial* input to the team, on day one and two, as described below. The best person is always someone who was in a previous learning team (see my website for details of current and previous teams: www.shirleyclarke-education.org) or who has a great deal of practical experience of formative assessment and is in tune with the principles of formative assessment outlined in this book (the practice can be varied, but the principles are set, proven from research). It is very useful to have other key people – such as advanced skills teachers or other advisors supporting the team – present on the days and available to make classroom visits.

Overview of the one-year project

Aims

- To form a learning team of teachers as action researchers, with an expectation that they will experiment with formative assessment in-between the project days and feed back their findings.

- To update teachers on recent, significant research findings which underpin effective formative assessment.

- To support teachers in reviewing and modifying existing practices and developing their professional confidence and expertise in the field, so that they can eventually lead others as a result of their learning.

- To share and celebrate achievement.

- Through dissemination of their feedback details via my website, to enable a wider range of teachers and pupils to benefit from the learning and impact of the work of the team.

DAY 1: Presentation of the following aspects of formative assessment

- *an effective learning culture*

- *learning objectives*

- *success criteria*

- *the importance of talk*

This day is mainly input, including discussion, tasks and video if possible. The whole project is first outlined, then the ultimate aims explained, and, for the rest of the day, current effective strategies used by teachers across the UK for the themes listed above are shared. These act as a starting point for teachers' own research.

Teachers are then asked to experiment with these themes and feed back their findings on the morning of Day 2. They are given a task sheet for their action research and some guidelines to focus their learning (see panel).

Learning Team Action Research Tasks after Day 1

By Day 2:

The 'growth' mindset

1. Experiment with the strategies suggested for developing a 'growth' mindset with your class/es. Talk to the pupils about it, modifying the elements for your age group.

Involving pupils in pre-planning

2. Before you do any detailed planning, **introduce the elements to be covered (knowledge and skills)** in a visual form and ask pupils what they already know about those things, what they would like to know and what they would like to be able to do. Create a **visual interactive display** to make future learning explicit, and use it to show new learning taking place. Do this with one unit of work only to begin with, then move on to another.

Learning objectives

3. In short-term plans, **separate the learning objective from the context for each lesson and, for knowledge learning objectives, link them with a key skill.** Do this in one subject only if this is new, then move to others. Make this separation explicit to pupils when introducing the learning objective (e.g. '*This is what we are learning and this is how we are going to learn it.*')

Success criteria

4. Plan **process success criteria** (what they will need to do in order to achieve the learning objective). Start with one subject only, and plan with someone if possible. Use web resources if you are not sure.

5. When introducing a learning objective for the first time, **pupils must generate the success criteria** for maximum effect. Use one of the following techniques, or your own ideas, for this to happen:

   - Give them a good finished example of the work they will be doing (writing, mathematics, art, PE video, etc) and ask what features they can see/what the thing consists of.
   - Show two contrasting pieces of finished work, as above, and ask which is best and why. The analysis via talk partners will generate the success criteria, by focusing on what the poorer example could include to be as good as the better example.
   - Get them to do one example first (if a repetitive exercise or skill for which the finished product does not reveal the success criteria), then tell you what steps they followed or needed to include.
   - Ask pupils '*Can you. . .?*' If yes, '*Prove it! What do I have to do first, next and so on?*'
   - Demonstrate how to create the finished product by doing everything wrong, so that the pupils have to correct you, thus creating the success criteria.

6. Have **talk partners/learning partners** as a constant feature of your lessons. Decide a random choosing technique and any other strategies discussed you want to experiment with, including your own ideas. Share the rationale for the whole thing with pupils and parents, emphasising that partners change every one or two weeks. Create talk-partner success criteria and use these for developing pupil awareness. Remember to avoid questions with 'hands up', but instead ask talk partners to discuss.

Remember to:
- Build on what you are already doing.
- Start slowly. . . one subject/one lesson at a time.
- Talk to each other about what you are doing – compare notes, plan together where possible.
- Jot down notes about things you've tried out and what happened.
- **Look for impact on pupils' learning, the evidence for this and your teaching**.
- Think of yourself as an action researcher – these are starting points or 'ways in': modify or experiment with your own ideas as you go along.

DAY 2: Feedback and presentation of remaining aspects of formative assessment

Morning: teacher feedback

The teachers are organised into five phase groups, the aim being that their discussions will be more useful if they talk to others working with similar age groups.

The morning then consists – for each of the themes teachers were asked to experiment with – of ten-minute focused discussions, followed by summary feedback to the team from a member of each group. Teachers are asked to focus their feedback on **the impact on the learning and the evidence they had for their claims,** rather than too much detail about what they did. For each issue, one teacher is the scribe/spokesperson. The feedback from each group leads to interesting discussion, and successes and problems are shared and examined (see below for more detail about the organisation of the morning).

Afternoon: input

Current effective practice focusing on:

- *effective questioning*

- *quality*

- *self/peer-assessment*

Teachers are then asked to experiment with these aspects and feed back their findings on the morning of Day 3. They are given a task sheet for their action research and some guidelines to focus their learning (below).

Learning Team Action Research Tasks after Day 2

By Day 3:
1. Continue trialling the ideas from before, building on Day 2 feedback and any of your own ideas.

Effective questioning
2. Experiment with changing recall questions into more worthwhile question formats: the range of answers, the statement, right and wrong, starting from the end, the opposing standpoint. Aim for your responses to build confidence rather than the opposite, avoiding subtle 'put downs'.

Discussing quality
3. With open skills, before pupils start to work, compare two pieces to demonstrate quality against one of the success criteria of today's lesson. Buy a flexi-cam or visualiser or use one of the suggested techniques. Make this a valuable teaching section of the lesson, and get the pupils involved through talk partners (*How does this bit fulfil the success criterion? How well has it been done? Now look at this person's work. How does it compare to the first in terms of the success criterion? Why is it better? Exactly? How could the first one be improved to make it as good as the second?*, etc.) **With writing, remember to focus on precise, small extracts rather than trying to compare huge pieces of work.**

Success and improvement *(best successes and where to improve)*
4. During lessons, stop the pupils and either (a) use an old piece of work to project and discuss or (b) choose one person's work (at random) to project at the front to discuss what has been done so far. The aim here is to teach *continual* review strategies, rather than stopping at the end when it is too late to affect the work in progress. **Do not read the work out – you will lose most of the impact of this process.**

Success and improvement consists of getting the class, in talk partners, to:
(a) Look for the one or two 'best bits' of the work. Although it is useful to begin by asking if the person's work has **included** the success criteria so far, the most important discussion will arise from identifying excellence (*Which bit/aspect is most effective/really stands out/do you like the best?*), as this builds up pupils' idea of quality. After sharing pupils' opinions, decide together the two best bits and highlight/circle/underline them on the projected work.
(b) Look for one part which could be improved. Again, get pupils to discuss and decide, and then highlight/underline/circle in a different colour the bit to be improved on the projected work. 'Improved' usually means changing something or extending it.

(c) In pairs, pupils do the improvement for the projected work and these are shared and one chosen to write on the projected work.

This process acts now as a model for pupils to do exactly the same thing on their own work, working together on each other's work in turn.

Summary

Aim for lessons/series of lessons to consist of:
- sharing long-term and short-term learning objectives;
- deciding success criteria, unless they have already been generated;
- demonstrating quality by comparing two pieces;
- checking their work against the criteria to make sure they are included;
- modelling success and improvement during lessons, followed by getting them to decide on their own success and improvement needs, working sometimes in pairs, sometimes alone, making improvements there and then;
- focus ends of lessons on discussions about successes identified and improvements made.

Teachers are also asked to start thinking about which area of formative assessment they are most interested in and would like to share findings about for the showcase event on Day 3.

Finally, teachers are asked to each produce an A1-sized poster for the showcase which will complement their presentation.

DAY 3: Feedback and showcase

Morning: teacher feedback 9:30–10:45 (tea break 15 mins) and 11:00–noon.

The teachers are again organised into five phase groups. As this is the autumn term, they will now be with their new year groups/classes, so the groups will have a different mix from Day 2.

The morning then consists of the same format as for the morning of Day 2.

Teachers are asked also to discuss any new ideas and findings since Day 2, and the impact of the project, and to summarise the changes in the culture of their classrooms.

Afternoon: the Showcase – the team plus 70 (max.) visitors from local schools.

If the project is being run with the entire staff of a single school only

Research shows that enlisting *all* the staff in a project causes some to feel coerced and hostile to yet more change. By far the best approach is to outline the project and ask for volunteers. A small team embarks on the project, reporting back to the staff at regular intervals. After a year, the whole staff is usually very willing and eager to take on the project as a school.

Teachers/teaching assistants need to be paired for the project, to provide a 'talk partner' to discuss the issues.

The person who does the input needs to be either an outside speaker, preferably from one of my learning teams, current or past, or a teacher skilled at formative assessment.

Interim meetings are easy to organise, and the showcase could be held within the school hall on a closure day.

Alternatively, the project can be run as input and feedback sessions, using three closure days over a year, with no showcase. However, the showcase does more than present the findings: it focuses the teachers on one aspect in depth and forces them to prepare a short presentation, working together as a small team to organise that presentation. The thinking involved, and the explanation required, takes their learning to a deeper level. Teachers are always slightly nervous on the day, but end up being exhilarated and ready to do it again, often complaining that they needed much more time to communicate all they had learnt.

More about the teacher feedback sessions

I have found the organisation of the feedback days is key to maximising the impact of the team. Most teachers come to Day 2 with a combination of success stories and things they have found difficult. It is in their small-group discussions that their successes get shared and passed on, and most problems get sorted out by the group. I believe that there would not be the same rich, frank exchange of ideas in this way if they thought an 'expert' or the project coordinator or other judgemental figure were listening to them or if they had to voice their problems in front of everybody. If the 'expert' is sitting with them – observing or, worse, joining in – there will be the same effect as if you were to sit with a group of children: they freeze, take a lead from the expert and say what they think you want them to say. They certainly don't find it easy to admit any difficulties.

The ingredients I have found most effective in running the feedback sessions are:

The groups

The teachers find it most helpful if their findings are discussed with teachers working with similar age groups, so get them into five groups of six people at the most – no more than five groups, or the feedback takes too long. Keep the numbers even across the groups so there is a fair chance for everyone to have their say – don't have three in one group and six in another. If there are fewer than 30 people, have fewer groups with even distribution – again, no more than five groups and as few people as possible in each group.

Itemise the feedback

Write up the key feedback topics for all to see – for example:

1. A growth mindset

2. Separating the learning objective from the context

3. Success criteria

4. Talk partners

Underneath this, show the order in which the groups will be feeding back, so that they don't feed back in the same order each time, with the last group always saying *'Everything has already been said . . . .'* I usually do the first round of feedback in age-group order (e.g. Nursery/Reception, Year 1/2, Year 3/4, etc), then for the second issue reverse order, then for the next two issues, random order. Give the groups numbers or letters:

1. A B C D E

2. E D C B A

3. C E A D B

4. D A B C E

Timings

It depends how long you have for the feedback session as to how long can be allowed, so my timings are based on a three-hour session with a 15-minute break.

Over the three hours, the four issues need to be discussed and feedback shared, with a little whole-team discussion when something needs it. I usually give the groups ten minutes each time to talk, then two minutes for the scribe to read out what they have written to their group, so that the group can modify it if it doesn't say what they wanted to say. It is a tricky task to be the scribe, so it is important to stress the joint responsibility of helping the scribe write what you want them to write. Then I allow about half an hour for the feedback. The half-day session looks like this, with a break in the middle, even if that falls in the middle of some feedback:

- **Coordinator** reads out issues to be discussed and reminds group what they mean (should not be necessary, but I always do it!) Then go over exactly how to share findings in those 10 minutes, as described below.

- **Focus one**: 10 minutes' discussion, plus 2 minutes going over their notes, then 30 minutes for all the groups to feed back.

- **Focus two**: the same, but new scribe/spokesperson.

- **Focus three**: the same, but new scribe/spokesperson.

- **Focus four**: the same, but new scribe/spokesperson.

Focusing the discussions

During their ten-minute discussions, the last thing you want is for the teachers to speak one after another around the table saying what happened in their class. This always results in running out of time, too many anecdotes and a focus on what was done rather than the impact on the learning. Instead, ask the teachers to focus their discussions on two things:

What was the impact of this particular aspect on pupils' learning?

How did you know this was the impact? (i.e. what took place to make you believe this to be true? What evidence did you have?)

I usually demonstrate how this might work (one person says 'Success criteria enabled my children to focus and self-evaluate'; the scribe writes this down and asks 'How did you know?'; the teacher describes what made her believe they were more focused, etc; the scribe then asks 'Did anyone else find the same effect?'; she writes what they say, sometimes as a tally, then asks, 'Did anyone find anything different happened?', and so on). If many people say the same thing, it needs to be noted for possible significance. If *every* group says it, we *know* it is significant. During the ten minutes, there will be some anecdotes, so it works well to ask for just one illustrative anecdote to be selected for each group feedback. The final feedback, therefore, for the whole team for each topic, will be five pieces of feedback with five illustrative anecdotes.

After the twelve minutes, ask the spokesperson/scribe for each group to read out their feedback in turn, stopping to hand over each time to the anecdote teacher, who will tell it to the whole team. The coordinator needs to interject if something needs to be said. My own comments are usually words of admiration, surprise if it is an unexpected finding, or questioning if it sounds as if we are moving away from the essence and ethos of formative assessment in some way.

Local authority action

Gateshead Local Authority (a learning team in 2004) produced a 'catalogue' of examples of formative assessment in action as a result of their action research. Fig. 11.1 reproduces a page which shows the detail of what could be possible in raising awareness of and implementing formative assessment in schools from an authority standpoint: the 'big picture'.

During my one-year project with East Lothian teachers, two educational psychologists and the coordinating headteacher, Ann McLanachan, evaluated the project's success and impact in the following ways:

- Initial evaluation questionnaire
- Before-and-after video analysis of a standard lesson
- Examination of before-and-after lesson documents
- Examination of evidence of reflective practice
- Questionnaire with P7 pupils (11 year olds)

Their full evaluation report to East Lothian Council (McLanachan, 2007) ended:

❝ This report concludes that the East Lothian Learning Team has been an excellent model for CPD (Continuing Professional Development). The initiative has had an extremely positive impact on the teaching and learning process in the represented schools.

'The model should be adopted as part of the strategic policy for Teaching and Learning and should be repeated and further developed in future academic year sessions as a priority. ❞

Spread Awareness

- Raise the awareness of headteachers and other senior leaders and key figures (send emails/letters/use briefing sessions).
- Bring to their attention articles in the TES and other sources which explain formative assessment, its potential and impact.
- Purchase the Black & Wiliam booklets Inside the Black Box and Working inside the Black Box and send to all schools. (there are other materials which may be useful to draw awareness or purchase and send).
- Draw attention to the work of practitioners who are developing learning through the use of formative assessment, e.g. Mary James, Shirley Clarke.

Ensure Involvement

- Use a development/improvement initiative with a focus to begin to impact upon standards of learning through the use of formative assessment procedures, eg. the use of a 'school intervention and support programme' with schools of concern.
- Pass on knowledge and understanding of formative assessment to Consultants and Advisory Teachers so that they use those approaches for learning with pupils in the classroom situation.
- Build open and trusting relationships with headteachers, assessment co-ordinators and other key figures and encourage them to: have in-service training for all staff on formative assessment systems and work alongside developing classroom practice. Target specific groups, subject areas and monitor the improvement. Create a learning climate within a culture and ethos which promotes learning and develops an ongoing dialogue of what learning is about and what is used successfully.

Raise the Profile

- Develop an Assessment Group, with interested and keen teachers, assessment co-ordinators; headteachers, meet regularly (about once per half term for 1 hour); share new ideas and developments; suggest trialing and reporting back.
- Put on conferences for assessment, try a different approach (e.g. 2 day conferences to focus and create reflection time and dialogue about assessment); let them be led by high profile key-note speakers known nationally and internationally; use appealing venues; publicise these well in advance - evaluate and follow through afterwards.
- Use Displays, in education centres/schools; use assessment models; use children's work sharing formative assessment producers; use quotes from formative assessment work.

Help to facilitate change

For some schools, focusing upon the improvement of learning through the use of formative assessment in particular may be a radical change to their approach. They need to reflect and alter their ethos and the culture of the place in which they work, so as to develop an atmosphere and climate which is conducive to improving learning; and where there is continuing dialogue about learning developments.

- Lead and manage change by offering to:
- Support schools by working alongside teachers in classrooms.
- Produce documentation with ideas and practice - which have been trialled and amended in Gateshead the Accessing Assessment document was produced after 2 years of trialing) to support schools who don't have direct local authority personnel working in school. Part of this development was used as a framework to develop formative assessment.
- Encourage the authority to conduct a type of mini audit which investigates examples of best practice, and then produce a booklet which collates reasons why formative assessment is working successfully; disseminate this information across the authority and beyond.
- Produce video material of pupils learning with the different stages of formative assessment.
- Take photographs and use on disk to illustrate presentations of good ideas in classroom use.
- Develop action research style projects, which encourage teachers to trial ideas with no pressure to 'get it right' critically reflect on what works, and share their findings, building on each others successful practice.
- Disseminate the action research findings through documentation/briefings and presentations/ in-service work/conference show-case events.
- Encourage headteachers and practitioners in their work by acknowledging and praising their success and involving them in disseminating the good practice in their schools.
- Build capacity for schools to be self sustaining in their learning improvements so that they ultimately become independent learning organisations

Extending Capacity

- Encourage schools' formative assessment systems and strategies of best practice for learning to be shared with secondary colleagues.

This may be facilitated through:
- Workshop type conferences, e.g. transfer/transition.
- Using strategy co-ordinators who can watch video material/listen to primary pupils and teachers talking about their approach to learning.
- Committing time for secondary year 7 staff to talk about approaches and systems with their primary year 6 colleagues from their feeder schools.
- Local authority consultants working with year 7 staff to ensure similar formative assessment practices will be carried into Key Stage 3 phase of learning.

Monitoring
- A joint monitoring approach between the schools to ensure systems and procedures are continued may be helpful to both parties.
- A feedback meeting would bring a more developed understanding to the use of formative systems in the development of learning.
- Pupils could be asked to report their views on whether formative assessment approaches have helped to improve their learning and how, and whether they have been consistent and continuous.
- Use peer coaching and coaching strategies with teachers who have a strong knowledge and understanding, so that they will coach others

Network - Sustaining Improvement

- With other authorities, eg. AAIA north-east is a strong platform to share best practice across a number of local authorities.
- Together produce video documentation exploring a specific aspect of the development of formative assessment, and share this amongst all schools. (AAIA north-east produced a document on 'Pupil Self-Assessment).
- Hold joint conferences with speakers who will help to give - formative assessment a high profile and move learning forward.
- Within the authority.
  - Primary schools whose practice is good can share with others and encourage development.
  - Use other existing systems to develop formative assessment such as the Consultant Leader programme.
  - Produce additional documentation which illustrates successful practice so that schools may adapt ideas.
  - Display materials on the local authority website.

Developing Formative Assessment in Gateshead Primary Schools

Lead Manage Develop

Encourage Sustainability Share

Enthuse Support

Build Capacity Improve

Fig. 11.1 Gateshead model for building capacity to improve learning and teaching (with thanks to Assessment Team of Gateshead, Raising Achievement Service)

If funding allows, it certainly would be worth putting some evaluation measures in place, if the action research model is to be used a number of times or if accountability exists beyond pupil achievement.

Supporting teacher development

The following extracts are from an extended account by Emma Goff, a member of the Tonbridge Learning Team in 2005, providing in-depth advice on ways of supporting teachers in developing their practice (visit the *Active Learning through Formative Assessment* page at www.hoddereducation.co.uk or www.shirleyclarke-education.org for the full article). She takes her experience with one school as a vehicle for illustrating the important steps and processes involved in creating effective change and enriching children's learning, without deskilling teachers or diminishing their confidence.

Working with teachers to support development in their own practice

Aim: to establish consistent use of formative assessment

When I was commissioned to work with a two-form-entry primary school whose priority was to establish consistent use of formative assessment across all year groups, it was an opportunity for me to share their vision. . . This proved to be an interesting discussion, as each of the people present had their own interpretations of what formative assessment was and what it looked like in their school. . . .

Building on current practice

Sharing success was an important stage in the process, as it confirmed the value of their existing practice. Asking open coaching questions enabled the teachers to reflect on the impact of this practice on children's learning. . . .

Investigating children's understanding

When we reflected on the lesson together, the teacher expressed concern that the children had not interpreted her objective in the way she had intended. Focusing on the children's responses during my interaction with the teacher enabled her to begin to consider ways of further supporting children's learning without devaluing her practice. . . .

Formalising instinctive good practice

. . .However, when reflecting specifically on use of formative assessment, the teacher found it difficult to identify what she'd done. Perhaps this was because her use of questioning and feedback was so embedded in her practice that it didn't seem obvious. Or maybe it was because the strategies she used were so personalised that they didn't bear a strong resemblance to her theoretical knowledge of assessment.

Establishing current systems
Sharing practice by working alongside teachers in a range of year groups provided evidence that formative assessment was used throughout the school even though it looked different in each class. . ... In order to establish a whole-school focus which was accessible at all levels, middle managers were involved in reflecting on the manageability and usefulness of systems that were currently in place to record assessments on a daily or weekly basis. . . . .

Prioritising one element of formative assessment: success criteria
Based on the available evidence, the teacher leading assessment in the school decided to prioritise introduction of success criteria as a way of making the process of learning explicit to children. . . . These explorations led to well-informed, subtle changes in their planning formats and later were used as models for other teachers.

The role of the mentor/advisor
In order to work successfully together with teachers to support this strategic focus, we assumed a shared responsibility for progress. Whilst the teacher was responsible for making small changes in the classroom based on evaluation and reflection, my role was to be an active listener to support the teacher's thought process . . . .

The development plan
Once a realistic baseline of current practice had been established during the autumn term, we began to write a long-term development plan. An overview of when formative assessment techniques would be introduced over a 2–3 year period was intended to support embedded practice rather than overload already busy teachers with too many changes.

The importance of teachers being 'action researchers'
Each technique was introduced at a whole-school staff meeting and then followed up at key stage and yeargroup meetings. As I continued to work alongside teachers in their classes, supporting reflections on their practice and challenging them to make decisions about their next steps, regular reviews and monitoring by senior leaders in the school supported an ongoing evaluation of the impact and progress of formative assessment strategies that were being established.

Helping teachers make choices
Focusing tightly on children's learning helped keep thinking on track. Active listening and careful questioning enabled me to establish a clear idea of what the teachers had achieved, and to support them in making their next steps with confidence.

The review process
Following observations of the use of success criteria as part of the school monitoring cycle, we planned a staff meeting during the summer term to review our progress. This was to be an opportunity for teachers to talk about their practice and evaluate the success of the strategies they had established. . . .. The debate generated from the insights shared was inspiring. . . .

Ways forward: using the developing expertise and keeping it going
We recognised that some teachers had confidence, commitment, enthusiasm and a very clear understanding of the concept of formative assessment, evidenced in coaching conversations, lessons observations and in planning. The assessment leader and I realised their potential to

support the next stage of our long-term plan and invited them to form a 'leading teachers' group for the school.

Supporting teachers in the early stages of development

Coaching and monitoring support continued alongside regular whole-school professional development and key stage meetings. This enabled me to focus on specific issues with individual teachers, to help them enrich learning opportunities for children. . . .

Extending teachers who have developed further

In classes where teachers were confident and secure with formative assessment, my role was to help them unpick what was making the difference to children's learning, e.g. 'What happened when you. . .?', 'How did the children respond to. . .?', 'What difference do you think it made when you. . .?'. . .

Empowered and autonomous

By the end of the autumn term, in the second year of commissioning, the leadership team at the school felt that they no longer needed additional support from an advanced skills teacher. Teachers had begun to take on more responsibility for effecting change and to ask their own questions as they widened the application of their skills and knowledge.

Emma Goff

The key elements of effective support

Effective support involves teachers learning not only about formative assessment, but also the role of pupils as learners and the importance of establishing a climate for learning.

The elements involved in developing formative assessment successfully in a school, empowering teachers to continue that development without support:

- Establishing aims and sharing interpretations of those aims.
- Celebrating existing success.
- Investigating pupils' understanding as a way to help teachers make changes without devaluing their practice.
- Formalising instinctive good practice by analysis.
- Creating long-term plans.
- Prioritising and focusing on one aspect of formative assessment only (the learning can usually be applied to other areas as a consequence).
- Sharing responsibility for pupils' progress and teachers' progress with teachers.
- Ask good coaching questions (e.g. 'What were you pleased to notice about the pupils' learning in this lesson?')
- Supporting teachers in the early stages differently to those who are further along.
- Conducting reviews by asking all those involved, especially the pupils.

In supporting teacher development, perhaps the greatest achievement possible is to enable teachers to reflect on their practice – firstly within a supportive working relationship, and then independently. Empowering professionals to have the confidence and autonomy to make their own decisions, and to value their own judgements, builds their capacity to raise standards and, most importantly, to instil in their pupils a love of learning and a love of challenge. This is our gift to our pupils: the best possible preparation for their lives ahead.

Final reflection

- How successful has professional development for formative assessment been so far in helping all teachers fully understand and embed its ethos, principles and strategies?
- Is there resistance to change by some people, regardless of how many meetings are held?
- Would action research, first carried out by a small group of volunteers who report their findings to the staff, be a feasible starting point?
- Have you surveyed teacher/heads' opinion about the best development model for developing formative assessment?
- How far are the key principles of formative assessment being followed in your classroom/department/school/authority?
    Is there a 'growth mindset' culture?
    Are pupils involved in preplanning discussions?
    Do teachers share decontextualised learning objectives?
    Are pupils able to transfer skills across the curriculum?
    Are success criteria pupil-generated?
    Are quality discussions a regular feature for open skills lessons?
    Do pupils have talk partners?
    Is there a 'no hands up' policy, where appropriate?
    Are questions designed for learning and thinking?
    Is self- and peer-assessment integrated in lessons and modelled?
- What have been your successes in formative assessment?
- Have you recognised them and celebrated them?

References

Alexander, R (2004) *Towards Dialogic Teaching*, Dialogos UK.

Assessment Reform Group (2002) *Assessment for Learning: Ten Principles* www.assessment-reform-group.org.uk.

Assessment Reform Group (2006) *The Role of Teachers in the Assessment of Learning* www.assessment-reform-group.org.uk.

Birmingham City Council (2007) *Effective Assessment: summarising, recording and tracking progress.*

Black, P. and Wiliam, D. (1998) 'Assessment and Classroom Learning', *Assessment in Education, 5, 1.*

Bloom, B. S. (1969) 'Some theoretical issues relating to educational evaluation', in R.W. Tyler (Ed.) *Educational evaluation: new roles, new means: the 63rd yearbook of the National Society for the Study of Education* (part II) (Vol. 69, 2, 26–50). University of Chicago Press.

Clarke, S. (2005) *Formative Assessment in Action: weaving the elements together,* Hodder and Stoughton.

Clarke, S. website for previous publications and Learning Team Updates: www.shirleyclarke-education.org

Claxton, G. (2002) *Building Learning Power,* TLO Limited, Bristol.

Crooks, T. (1988) 'The impact of classroom evaluation processes on students', *Review of Educational Research, 58,* 1–14.

De Bono, E. (1999) *Six Thinking Hats,* Penguin

DFES (2003) *Excellence and Enjoyment: a Strategy for Primary Schools,* London, DfES.

Dweck, C. (1975) 'The role of expectations and attributions in the alleviation of learned helplessness', *Journal of Personality and Social Psychology, 31,* 674–685.

Dweck, C. (1989) 'Motivation', in A. Lesgold and R. Glaser, *Foundations for a Psychology of Education,* Hillsdale, NJ: Erlbaum.

Dweck, C. (2006) *Mindset: The New Psychology of Success,* Random House.

Dweck, C. (2000) *Self-theories: their role in motivation, personality and development,* Psychology Press.

Elliott, E. and Dweck, C. (1988) 'Goals: an approach to motivation and achievement', *Journal of Personality and Social Psychology, 54,* 1, 5–12.

Fisher, R (1996a) 'Thinking skills', in Arthur, J., Grainger, T., and Wray, D. (Eds) *Learning to Teach in Primary School,* Routledge Falmer.

Fisher, R. (1996b) *Stories for Thinking*, Oxford: Nash Pollock.

Hargreaves, D.H. (2004) *Personalised Learning 2: student voice and assessment for learning*, London: Specialist Schools Trust.

Hind, A. (2007) From a talk given at the AAIA (Assessment and Improvement Association) conference in Newcastle in September 2007.

Lepper, M.R. and Hodell, M. (1989) 'Intrinsic Motivation in the Classroom', in C.Ames and R.Ames, *Research on Motivation in Education* (Volume 3), Acadmic Press.

Lipman, M. (2003) *Thinking in Education*, Cambridge University Press.

McLanachan, A. (2007) *Learning Teams Project: Summary Document*, East Lothian Council.

Mercer, N. (2000) *Words and Minds; how we use language to think together*, Routledge.

Natriello, G. (1987) 'The impact of evaluation processes on students', *Educational Psychologist, 22*, 2, 155–75.

Pardoe, D. (2005) *Towards Successful Learning*, Network Educational Press/Continuum.

Sadler, R. (1989) 'Formative assessment and the design of instructional systems', *Instructional Science, 18*, 119–44.

Scriven, M. (1967) *The Methodology of Evaluation* (Vol.1), American Educational Research Association.

SEAL (Social and Emotional Aspects of Learning) www.DCSF.gov.uk

Smith, A. and Call, N.(1999) *The ALPS Approach: Accelerated Learning in Primary Schools*, Network Educational Press.

Weiner, B. (1984) 'An attribution theory of achievement motivation and emotion', *Psychological Review, 92*, 548–73.

Weiner, B., Heckhausen, H., and Meyer, W. (1972) 'Causal ascriptions and achievement behaviour: A conceptual analysis of effort and a reanalysis of locus of control', *Journal of Personality and Social Psychology, 21*, 239–48.

Wiliam, D. (2006) 'Assessment for Learning: why, what and how', edited transcript of a talk given at the Cambridge Assessment Network Conference on 15 September 2006 at the Faculty of Education, University of Cambridge.

Wiliam, D. and Thompson, M. (2006) 'Integrating assessment with learning: what will it take to make it work?', in Dwyer, C. A. (Ed.) *The Future of Assessment: Shaping Teaching and Learning*, Lawrence Erlbaum Associates.

Vygotsky (1978) *Mind in Society*, Harvard University Press.